Search for a Latin American Policy

Search for a
Latin American Policy

by

THOMAS W. PALMER, JR.

UNIVERSITY OF FLORIDA PRESS

GAINESVILLE — 1957

PRINTED BY FLORIDA GROWER PRESS, TAMPA, FLORIDA

BOUND BY UNIVERSAL-DIXIE BINDERY, INC., JACKSONVILLE, FLORIDA

Introductory Note

I am extremely happy to have the opportunity to write an introductory note to this volume. Having just returned from a trip to Latin America and having reread Professor Palmer's well-rounded manuscript, I am more than ever aware of its importance. I know of no other work that gives a clearer idea of the significance of the republics to the south of us in our foreign relations, or a more interesting and penetrating picture of the problems that we face there at the present time. Professor Palmer had not only drive and enthusiasm but a singularly mature and well-balanced judgment. His practical experience, united with his scholarly training and habits, has resulted in a book of very high value. His untimely death is a real loss to the cause of inter-American understanding. But this able treatise is a fitting memorial.

Cornell University   DEXTER PERKINS

Foreword

Dr. Palmer chose a difficult and intriguing subject when he set out to write *Search for a Latin American Policy*. An answer to the questions raised calls for the wide learning of a scholar and the wisdom of a statesman. The problem of what, in the light of the national interest, would be good United States policy toward the nations that lie south of our border poses the question: What is the national interest and how best serve it? No question is more challenging or more difficult, and no one I think has dealt with it with a better sense of what is possible than has the author in this wise and restrained book. The reader will discover for himself the perceptive quality of insight that enables the author to mark out the limits within which policy must operate and beyond which it becomes a self-defeating gesture.

The work will be characterized by critics as a study in realism. For the hard realities that shape policy are clearly evident. But it is a realism informed by a deep sympathy with the needs and difficulties of the people of Latin America and an awareness of their urge to shape the world to fit their own notions of right and good. This quality of sympathetic insight and awareness of the bounds set by resource, tradition, history, and the arts that control contemporary strategic considerations give the study a special kind of validity and the particular quality of restraint spoken of before.

The position of "strategic loneliness" occupied by Latin America circumscribes its relative place in over-all United States policy considerations. Our policy towards Latin America must fit into the wider realm which includes Asia, Africa, the Near East, Europe, and Russia. In so complex and politically unstable a world the national interest dictates a universal perspective. Within these broad limits our relations with Latin America can develop special objectives derived from good neighborliness or dictated by the special needs of the people in the area and by their particular possibilities in peace and war.

But the author is aware, as few students have been, that in a complex culture changes are slow and that the flaws and the failings on both sides of the border have a way of surviving good intent and pious wishes. No one I think will lay down the book without a sense of gratitude for the deeper understanding which will have come to him. And, if any part of the volume is to be singled out, the chapters on Guatemala and Bolivia will prove doubly revealing for their objectivity and insight.

The sudden death of Dr. Palmer makes this the final testament to a highly promising career of scholarship and public service.

Columbia University   FRANK TANNENBAUM

Preface

This study grew out of my increasing conviction that the need for a critical appraisal of the role of Latin America in United States foreign policy is acute. Numerous works have appeared in recent years on foreign policy toward Europe, Asia, and the Near East, but none on the Latin American area as a whole. It is distressing that so little serious attention has been devoted to this rapidly growing region of more than 170 million people. The basic reasons for taking Latin America largely for granted are examined in the first chapter of this book. While the conclusions reached do not give grounds for great optimism, it is to be hoped that at least some perceptible increase in long-range thinking about Latin America will take place in the next few years. In addition to many specific suggestions along the way, a few broad guidelines for orientation of future policy are given at the end.

It should be made clear that this book is not a history of United States policy toward Latin America, though it does call to mind some of the lessons of earlier years. Nor does it attempt a comprehensive coverage of all phases of recent and contemporary United States-Latin American relations. Instead, it concentrates on those phases which appear to be of the greatest significance. The work is intended to be provocative, and to suggest further exploration of the lines of inquiry marked out.

An effort is made to maintain a responsible, balanced point of view, for example on such controversial subjects as dictatorship versus democracy in Latin America, United States policy toward dictatorships, and the performance and role of American private enterprise. Nonetheless, as a citizen of the United States I write with the enlightened national interests of my country as the paramount consideration. I firmly believe that these interests not only *are compatible with, but also beneficial to, those of the Latin American nations. Indeed I believe that a policy which is not based on these interests, but instead either on entirely self-centered considerations, or on purely idealistic ones of a "lyrical" Pan-Americanism, will in the end be self-defeating.*

A partial list of the bibliography from which I have drawn for my information and some of my ideas is given at the end. The statistical data are drawn largely from the New York Times and the official publications mentioned at the conclusion of the bibliography. I have also drawn to a great extent upon my government experience in Latin American work, particularly in 1951-1952 in Brazil with the Joint Brazil-United States Economic Development Commission.

It would take up entirely too much space to list the many people who have stimulated my thinking on inter-American relations. My colleagues in government work, both in Latin America and in Washington, have given me many ideas. So also have the scholars who have attended the meetings of the American Historical Association and the Council for Latin American Affairs. Provocative discussions with graduate students at Boston University and The Fletcher School of Law and Diplomacy have contributed materially. My original inspiration to enter the field of Latin American Studies came from my study at Columbia University under Frank Tannenbaum. My father, Thomas W. Palmer, a "gringo lawyer" of many years' experience, has helped me retain what I hope is a note of realism in my work.

T. W. P., JR.

Contents

-I-

Yankee Images of Latin America

Many readers may find this chapter an odd one with which to initiate a foreign-policy study. One might well argue, for example, that Chapter II, on the importance of Latin America to the United States, should come first. It might be wise at the outset, then, to explain the significance of this chapter and the reason for according it priority.

Latin America has largely been taken for granted by the United States in recent years. While various factors account for this, the most important basic one is a long-enduring climate of American* opinion of apathy, combined with amusement and condescension toward Latin America. In contrast to the attitudes toward Western Europe, there is no general framework of well-informed opinion to which people have recourse in their thinking. Most of the older generation of American intelligentsia, both in academic life and outside it, studied for some time in Europe. Naturally their cultural orientation has been permanently directed towards an admiration and esteem for certain European countries, usually the United Kingdom, France, Germany, or Italy. Even the younger generation continues to make its quest of foreign culture in Western Europe. Perhaps it will continue to do so in our lifetime, although there are gradually increasing numbers of geographical deviationists.

Now the general climate of public opinion toward a foreign area

---

*Throughout this book citizens of the United States will be referred to as "Americans" or "Yankees," and "American" interests will mean those of the United States. The term "North Americans," logically used by Latin Americans, is not employed, because this is not the way in which Americans customarily refer to one another. It might be noted that Latin Americans also use the term "Yanquis."

1

over a long period cannot help having a substantial impact on the thinking of foreign-policy formulators. Obviously other factors also weigh heavily: strategic and economic considerations, for example. Yet it goes without saying that the close bonds between the United States and Europe derive much of their cement from the understanding and sense of community that countless Americans have had for years with the motherlands. But when we turn to Latin America, we find that so far such bonds have been almost nonexistent. Indeed, by tending to color their thinking toward their southern neighbors adversely Americans' general ignorance and lack of real contact with Latin America have given rise to unfortunate images. What are these images?

Perhaps the most vivid impression, retained from childhood, is the one created by comic books and movies, and also, though to a lesser extent, by radio and television programs. Generally one pictures the lands to the south as peopled by bandits, indolent peasants, good-natured roustabouts who tag along after American cowboys and adventurers, beautiful *señoritas,* and occasionally helpful but corrupt government officials. With the exception of two or three good films on Mexico and one on Cuba, no Hollywood movies have appeared on serious themes involving Latin American history or politics. Yet the great epic of the Spanish conquistadores, the brilliant life and exploits of Simón Bolívar and San Martín, and other events and individuals should certainly provide rewarding material for Hollywood movie producers.

The more mature Yankee image would have the following principal features: Latin America is composed of a series of countries with primarily tropical climates, steaming jungles, and high mountains. These countries are peopled mostly by Indians, Negroes, and others of various racial mixture, with a number of upper-class whites in a few big cities such as Buenos Aires, São Paulo, Santiago, and Mexico City. They are for the most part a turbulent lot, excitable, sensitive, and politically intractable. Their leaders are strong on long-winded oratorical debates and weak on sustained constructive action. Revolts and counterrevolts, generally based purely on personal or at most factional quarrels, are the warp and

2

woof of their political pattern. Latin American governments are unstable and corrupt and are generally dominated by strong men who succeed one another in quasi-gangsterish fashion. The upper classes look down upon the lower-class laborers and peons (symbolized by the sleepy Mexican peasant with his broad sombrero). These plutocrats tend to invest their wealth in real estate and apartment buildings instead of in productive, socially useful enterprises. Furthermore, they are prone to excessive procrastination. There are great potentialities in some of these countries that could be realized if only Anglo-Saxons and northern Europeans had settled them, or at least could be allowed to enter now on favorable terms with large-scale private investments.

This second image, though obviously containing some partial truths, is not one causing most Americans to regard Latin America with respect. At best, it creates a feeling of benevolent paternalism or missionary and educational enterprise; at worst, it breeds an ill-concealed air of superiority, disdain, and impatience. Latin America's seeming inability to achieve stability and rapid progress becomes a distracting annoyance for the United States, which is busy with the "really important" foreign areas in contemporary world affairs.

Fully as serious in its impact on the attitudes of most thoughtful Americans is their view of Latin American cultural and intellectual achievements. With the partial exception of Mexico, most well-informed people have practically no contact with or understanding of Latin American culture. Ask an average group of college students in what ways Latin American culture has made any impressions on them, and they are likely to reply that popular dance music is the only one. A few might add Mexican art and archaeology, as depicted occasionally in popular magazines. Rare are the Americans who have ever read a work of literature by a Latin American essayist, poet, novelist, historian, or social scientist; few have ever heard of one. Almost total ignorance prevails regarding any past or contemporary scientific, mathematical, or philosophical contribution. Most significantly perhaps, it is hard to think immediately of any way in which Latin America has contributed to the

3

cultural heritage of the United States for example, in terms of political or philosophical ideas.

A partial exception to the general nationwide ignorance of Latin America can be made for those few parts of the United States bordering on Mexico and the Caribbean, where there are active trade interests, spoken Spanish, and certain university circles oriented perceptibly toward our southern neighbors. The best examples are the Miami and New Orleans areas and certain sections of Texas, New Mexico, and southern California. Even there the principal emphasis is on Mexico, or on Cuba in the case of Miami. It seems fairly safe to say that, if Mexico is excepted, there is practically no significant, enduring contact with Latin American culture and thought among well-educated circles in the United States.

Now there is no point in merely complaining about these views and about the general lack of attention to Latin America. The point is that these are the sober facts, and any consideration of relations with Latin America must recognize them. More important, they help to explain why Latin America has been taken for granted, why more serious attention has not been concentrated on the area.

In the light of the Good Neighbor Policy and wartime wooing of Latin America, the inattention of the last decade seems startling. It comes as a particular blow to younger Latin Americanists in the United States, who after starting to sail with a strong wind now find themselves becalmed or even in some instances stranded on the rocks. Yet the lack of interest is a complex phenomenon. Certainly there is no real hostility toward Latin American affairs. To the contrary, there seems to be a kind of passive acceptance of the fact that Latin America is "growing more important" and of the consequent need for more attention. Many people these days express the feeling that there is an upsurge of general interest in the area. One may be allowed to hope this is true; yet the evidence indicates that, once removed from the headlines, Latin America also drops out of mind for most people—until the next headlines. On balance a slight gain does appear to have been made, but as yet it is insubstantial. Yet why do not Americans have greater interest (except for Mexico) in twenty countries in their own hemisphere, having a combined total population already larger than that of the United States and growing faster than that in any other major region of the world—an area with an interesting, colorful history and breath-taking tourist attractions?

The reasons for this paradox probably originate in the handicaps from which Latin America suffers. One is geographical. A glance at the map at the front of this book reveals that, though Mexico and the Caribbean area are close by, the major countries of South America are far removed from the main Western European-North American trade routes and political and strategic axes. Fully as important, they have thus far been prohibitively distant both in time and expense for the great bulk of American tourists. Furthermore, in contrast to Europe and Mexico, most of South America has not yet facilitated tourist document requirements nor constructed adequate hotels and travel facilities within its interior. The result is not surprising; in 1954-1956 only about 3 per cent of American tourists abroad visited South America. Though personal contact with a foreign region does not automatically lead to greater understanding of it, an almost complete lack of such contact does make understanding more difficult. This is particularly true for an area about which there are not hundreds of government analysts, journalists, writers, and academicians constantly writing, studying, and evaluating, as they do, for example, about the Soviet Union, Communist China, or India.

But there are other important reasons for neglect besides geography. Latin America has not played a vital role in world power politics. During certain periods, European powers and the United States have been interested in it for colonial, economic, or certain other reasons, but its role has largely been that of a pawn. Only revolutionary Mexico and Peronist Argentina have thrust themselves dramatically forward. Since the end of the revolution's "Jacobinist" phase in 1938, Mexico has assumed a quieter role. The place as a major "trouble spot" was taken by Argentina with its challenges to the United States at Pan-American conferences, its pro-Axis role during most of World War II, and its subsequent attempts to achieve a "third position" between the Soviet Union and the United States. One might also add now its increasingly significant economic relationships with Germany and the Soviet Union. In recent years then, only Argentina has had even a limited *active* impact on world power politics, though if gigantic Brazil can realize its true economic potential, it should overshadow its southern rival. The struggles and revolts in the other nations of Latin America have been of little significance to the rest of the world.

In all fairness, it should be remembered that the United States interested Europe in the nineteenth century only because of its intriguing revolutionary experiment in democratic government, embodying the ideals of the Encyclopedists, and as a destination for emigrants. The American-proclaimed Monroe Doctrine was enforced largely by the British navy. By way of contrast, in this century the United States, Western Europe, Russia, India, China, and Japan have all played and are now playing dynamic parts in world struggles. Only now, and partly because of its recent Asian experience, is the United States slowly beginning to apprehend a greater meaning for Latin American developments and trends.

Like Asia relatively unknown, Latin America has not appeared to most Americans to be so exotic or mysterious. The exploration of Aztec and Inca ruins and the syncretism of pagan Indian beliefs with Roman Catholic Christianity have held fascination for a few. Also to some fortune hunters Latin America has appealed as a land of adventure and a place to get rich quick, and Mexico and Central America certainly have "vacation appeal." Most of Latin America, however, particularly the great population clusters and economically transforming communities of South America's east coast, has exercised neither the magnetic pull of oriental cults nor the attraction of the Near Eastern cradle of civilization. When writers and scholars turned their attention away from the history and culture of the major Western areas, their tendency was to look toward the East. This was due in part to the interrelationships and conflicts of Western Europe in these more remote regions. Of late, there has been a slight surge of interest among research

6

scholars in tropical Africa, where there is the novel attraction of a dark and unknown continent beginning to stir with restlessness.

Meanwhile Latin America continues to be regarded by many as merely an offshoot of Western civilization, more specifically of Latin Europe, without any significant philosophy or culture of its own, a kind of stepchild. Again Mexico must be partially excepted. Overlooked is the fact that though Latin America is geographically an integral unit of our Western civilization, it does have striking elements of cultural differentiation from the other parts of the West. Indeed, so-called "Mestizo America" has some cultural similarities with the East, as F. S. C. Northrop pointed out in his chapter on Mexico in *The Meeting of East and West.* On the other hand, since the conquest and achievement of independence there have been (except partially in Mexico) no great European-style developments or trends, no apparent bases for masterful syntheses like the *Rise of Modern Europe* series. This is obviously not to say that important, even exciting, developments have not been and are not today taking place throughout Latin America, but they are of quite a different magnitude and character from those which have taken place in Europe.

While Asian history has also been quite different from that of Europe, a substantial American missionary interest has, for one thing, helped to give a great impetus to the establishment of universities and historical and area studies. Missionaries have also done much fine educational work in Latin America, but a comparable area and university development simply has not appeared. Quite recently, political scientists and sociologists in the United Nations, foundations, and universities have become interested in political colonialism, which affects Asia and Africa far more importantly than it does Latin America. Thus culturally Latin America has on the whole been at a disadvantage with other foreign areas in competing for the attention and interest of thoughtful people in the United States.

The above are long-range considerations. There are, however, some important short-range factors which tended in the years following World War II to decrease general interest in the southern

7

republics. In the period 1938-1944, Latin America was "oversold" to the American public. The tremendous interest and enthusiasm for things Latin American evidenced by large segments of American society were wonderful to behold while they lasted. Spanish clubs were formed throughout the country; commercial products were given Latino names. At a more serious level an amazingly large number of academicians and government workers were drawn temporarily into inter-American work, most of them through Nelson Rockefeller's Office of the Coordinator of Inter-American Affairs. Then in 1944 all collapsed, and after the war, most of the foreign-minded public, able to return to European haunts, forgot Latin America.

Even more damaging was the tendency of many serious-minded academic people and government workers to react scornfully against the Latin American idea. A number of academicians who had been impressed with idyllic stories of the eagerness for progress of our "good neighbors" returned disillusioned from cultural and Point Four assignments to the south. While most "hard-core" Latin America specialists remained in the field, the effects of these adverse reactions were certainly damaging to both the scholarly and current affairs interests. A few years ago, at one major eastern university, a student intending to write a thesis on modern Argentina was advised to bring himself "abreast of the times" and choose a topic on some other area of greater world significance!

Some reaction against an emphasis on hemispheric solidarity has also taken place because, unfortunately and incorrectly, it came to be associated with isolationism. In the years before World War II, many of those who were strongly opposed to any involvement in European affairs favored hemispheric defense and closer relations with our neighbors. After the war, leading American statesmen turned practically their entire attention to safeguarding national security interests first in Europe and later in Asia. The few pro-ponents of greater emphasis on Western Hemisphere relations were regarded with some suspicion as neo-isolationists. The fact that some diehards have indeed continued to stress hemispheric interests exclusively should not lead anyone to suppose that a significant number of genuine Latin Americanists have at any time been hemispheric isolationists.

As is implied above, one of the major factors militating against attention to Latin America is the fact that since the Second World War it has not been a "crisis" area for the United States. Attention has been concentrated on regions nearer the center of Communist power. South America has seemed remote from transpolar and other likely bombing routes. Furthermore, the change of enemy from the Axis powers to the Soviet bloc meant that the United States need not worry about one important matter that earlier had concerned it. The large numbers of German and Italian business interests and citizens in Latin America had seemed either an actual or potential fifth column. In contrast, the Soviet bloc has had practically none of this type of direct involvement, and in fact those Latin American nationals of Russian, East European, and Chinese descent appear on the whole to be strongly anti-Communist. In view of the seeming remoteness from danger of Latin America, a few escapists have even looked longingly at the central part of Brazil as a refuge from the horrors of a mutually destructive atomic war. The area has been envisioned as one that might be spared a holocaust, wherein civilization might once again flourish. The interior of Brazil would thus assume the favored position which Toynbee has suggested for Central Africa.

Not until 1954, when the Guatemalan anti-Communist revolt erupted, did a large number of American citizens become genuinely concerned over the possibility that serious situations may arise in Latin America to threaten the security interests of the United States. Until then, the American press had on the whole given minimal coverage of Latin American news. It is doubtful that more than a handful of well-informed citizens could mention any significant postwar events in Latin America, other than the Peróns' activities and the 1948 riot at Bogotá during the Pan-American Conference. After the Guatemalan revolt, articles on Latin America appeared in profusion. While the headlines soon vanished, public interest since then does not seem to have returned to the completely apathetic state. Recent news of an unusually sensational character, including presidential assassinations and a suicide and the invasion of a Central American country, has helped to keep Latin America a little more in the press and the public eye.

It seems to take sensational, violent—one might say negative—news about Latin America to focus attention on it. To a certain degree this is true for all foreign news. In the case of Europe and Asia, however, a fairly large number of people carefully and persistently study constructive progress and even routine developments, which help give a balanced perspective. News presenting the affirmative, more attractive side of Latin America is rare, although special mention should be made of the valuable background articles in the *New York Times,* the *Christian Science Monitor, Time,* and one or two other publications. The press may well argue that it must give news about areas in which the public is more interested. The fact remains that most well-informed Americans are merely sporadically aware of Latin American developments, and then only of the violent, adverse, or perhaps comical type.

Another difficulty in obtaining a clear image of Latin America is that the impressions which Americans get from the accounts of both fellow-countrymen and Latin Americans are fragmentary. In view of the tremendous size of the area, the large number of countries, the widely differing geography, and the sharply varying degrees of economic and social progress, this is not surprising. Consider the impressions of Latin America conveyed by travelers who have visited respectively Mexico City and its Indianist environs, Europeanized Buenos Aires, ancient Inca ruins in Peru, the Chilean lake region, business-like São Paulo, the Amazon, Bolivia with its Point Four agricultural program, and Americanized Havana. One can hardly imagine more bewildering contrasts! Indeed some have questioned whether "Latin America" is a valid concept at all. Yet notwithstanding the differentiations and contrasts, there does seem to be something called Latin America, with basic similarities underlying most of its constituent parts.

An interest in knowing more about foreign peoples is more easily aroused if one feels he has something in common with them.

Clearly many Americans feel this way toward Europe and Canada, but a paradox appears in the case of Latin America. Despite the fact that both Yankees and Latins are "New Worlders" in the same hemisphere, how much do they feel that they really have in common? Ask an educated citizen of Lima, Ohio, how much he has in common with a citizen of Lima, Peru. He may be hard pressed to find any similarity other than that both live in countries that were once under European dominion, but that are now Western Hemisphere republics free from foreign control. Possibly he might be conscious that much of the wool, copper, aluminum, lead, and zinc in his garments and utensils comes from Latin America. Now anyone will admit that these bonds by themselves are not sufficient to create a community of interests. The difficulty is that there are hardly any similarities in the ways of life of the two citizens. Standards of living, economic environments, social structures, business mores, climatic conditions, political frameworks, cultural interests, and religious customs (even though both may be Roman Catholics)—all differ significantly. Although a few people in Ohio may well have a great interest in and understanding of Peru, the fact remains that there is a lack of basic sense of common interests and outlook with Peruvians. The group of historians now attempting to write an integrated history of the Americas will certainly have to contend with these hard facts.

Clearly the material issued by the Pan American Union to assist in the observation of Pan-American Day (April 14) is intended to produce in Yankees a community of interest with Latin America. Some of the specific items included for 1955 were "Sixty-five Years of Inter-American Cooperation"; "What the OAS [Organization of American States] is Today"; and leaflets giving views on inter-American cooperation as reflected in speeches of statesmen of the Americas. These obviously interest students of international organization, but the average American probably feels more of a sense of community with the United Nations than with the OAS. Of greater personal interest to most are some of the remaining items: an "Introduction to Latin American Countries Series," a map of the Pan-American Highway, a selection of popular Latin American

11

dances and recordings, with instructions for basic steps, and typical Latin American recipes. The easiest method to learn Spanish might have been added, a topic of as great concern to people with a potential interest in Latin America as any other. It is through media such as language, popular music, and travel that Americans may begin to acquire a greater insight into the Latin American way of life and its outlook toward them.

Before one leaves this problem, mention should be made of the Point Four program. To be realistic, it is hard for most Americans (or nationals anywhere) to have an active personal interest in and sympathy with the proverbial poor of distant lands. Most Yankees have no personal ties with underprivileged people in the so-called less developed countries. Nevertheless, the substantial technical-assistance ventures in which United States citizens are working shoulder to shoulder with Latin American nationals are the most concrete manifestation of inter-American cooperation at the working level. During his experience with a Point Four mission to Brazil, the author was continually impressed by the spectacle of American and Brazilian pioneers collaborating on health, agricultural, vocational education, and other projects. Here a community of interest definitely exists. Unfortunately only a small minority of Americans can participate in it, but at least it could serve as an example with which to illustrate common goals and purposes.

We have seen, then, that those interested in our country's foreign relations have a somewhat blurred or fragmented image of Latin America. We have also seen how the general lack of any real sense of common personal interests and relationships with our southern neighbors strongly inhibits the achievement of a greater understanding of Latin America. We have conceded that Latin America has not had for erudite Americans an attraction comparable even to that of Asia. Finally we have pointed up the obvious fact that in the postwar years Latin America has not been a "crisis" area and therefore has received much less attention from harassed foreign-policy makers than have most other global areas.

Fortunately, this is not the entire picture. An active, well-informed interest in Latin America and inter-American relations does exist

12

among four specific groups in our population: government employees, academic specialists, a handful of journalists and free-lance writers, and business circles. Though these groups naturally do not see exactly the same Latin American image, they agree fairly generally on most of the realities and problems. They scrutinize developments, trends, and American policies, and publish articles, pamphlets, and, less frequently, books on Latin American and inter-American topics.

Most of the comparatively few United States government employees concerned primarily with Latin American affairs have an excellent background of study in the area. They are able to follow perhaps more carefully than any of the other groups the contemporary political, economic, social, and international trends in Latin America. Unfortunately most of their analyses, since they must be classified, do not directly affect public thinking on Latin America. Furthermore, one gets the impression that top-level consideration of underlying Latin American trends and long-range American policies toward the area is sporadic. One even suspects that policies toward Latin America are often formulated on the basis of contacts between high-level officials and businessmen acquainted with Latin America and on personal impressions gained from "field trips," rather than from the carefully pondered views of working-level analysts in Washington. Now it may well be that occasionally on-the-spot assessment of situations by practical men of action is of more value than that of the detached, "ivory tower" thinker, though the latter is ostensibly better trained to weigh the various kinds of information. In any event, if this happens very often, the analyst may become discouraged. This, together with the general climate of opinion in Washington regarding Latin America as a "low priority" area, has caused a number of able, career-minded young men and women to regard specialization unfavorably in that area. Yet the fact remains that these government officials probably have the most accurate, over-all image of Latin America, and by virtue of their positions do exercise some influence over United States government policies.

For academic specialists, the situation is different. The number

13

of university faculty members specializing in Latin American, and especially United States-Latin American, affairs has declined in recent years. Today they represent only a very small percentage of the social-studies and humanities staffs in the majority of American colleges and universities. Included in this small group are a number of fine scholars, who have had years of experience in the Latin American area, who know Spanish and Portuguese well, and who have published a number of textbooks, monographs, and scholarly articles. Unfortunately most of these monographs and articles are too specialized for the reading public at large. Moreover, since comparatively few of them are concerned with contemporary developments and trends, they have little direct impact on the analyses and formulations of government policy toward Latin America. Yet it is through these scholars that our deeper cultural and intellectual understanding of Latin America is preserved.

Only a handful of American journalists and free-lance authors concentrate on Latin America. Apart from the journalists on the staffs of the *New York Times* and the *Christian Science Monitor*, it is difficult to recall more than one or two. In our national capital, not a single newspaper has a writer who specializes on Latin America. Quantitatively, the same is true for free-lance authors; books of a general, semipopular nature, with only two or three significant exceptions, have virtually disappeared from bookstores during the last several years. The few journalists and writers who do concern themselves with Latin America deserve credit and encouragement. They have important advantages over both the previously mentioned groups in that they keep up to date by travel throughout the area and are both free and willing to write on current events in Latin America, thereby reaching the general reading public. Naturally deadlines must be met; coverage must be short, readable, and concentrated primarily on events of the moment, thus running the risk of missing some of the underlying factors. Even so, the performance of the more highly qualified journalists has been notable.

Last, but by no means least, are the business circles with Latin American connections. Here a contrasting picture in terms of relative numbers presents itself. In most of the larger port cities,

14

and in some others, there is a fairly sizable number of business men keenly interested in Latin American developments. They operate in groups such as the National Foreign Trade Council, the International Chamber of Commerce, export clubs, and other business entities, all of which follow closely events south of the border. Together with a few civic-minded people, they sponsor Pan-American societies which provide social activities for the Latin American colonies and speakers on Latin American topics.

In the past and even now, certain business segments have not seen the Latin American political, economic, and social complex as a whole. Instead they have concentrated on short-range investment and trade interests, which is understandable in view of their concern over the large material stakes in Latin America. In recent years, however, most large American concerns operating in Latin America have tended to take a longer-range view of their own interests and have revealed more understanding of the underlying nationalistic political and social pressures and aspirations. Investment and banking concerns have found it necessary in their forecasts to take into consideration intangible political and social factors. They have discovered that the problems of remitting one's profits from a Latin American country are tied up with political trends and social policies, sometimes even with such seemingly unrelated factors as orientations in Latin American university courses. The employees of these concerns stationed in Latin America are now on the whole better prepared psychologically to work there, though much improvement is still needed in language and cultural backgrounds. By virtue of their large material stake and personal contact with the area, their not inconsiderable number, and their intense, dynamic interest in current developments, American businessmen can have a major impact on our relations with Latin America. As business ties with our southern neighbors inevitably increase, the numbers of Americans who come to know them through business eyes will increase correspondingly.

Latin America, unlike Europe and perhaps most of Asia and the Near East, is a pioneer area, where there is still room for considerable individual, uncoordinated initiative. It does seem imperative,

15

however, to bring increasing numbers of American businessmen together with governmental and academic specialists on Latin America in order to work out a common outlook on problems and policies. We are not suggesting a monolithic uniformity of the statist type, but rather the formation of an expanding nucleus of well-informed Americans who take Latin America more seriously, and who feel that both government and business should have *some* long-range policies toward it, even if they may disagree on particulars.

These people will do well to ponder two vital questions: (1) In precisely what ways is Latin America important to the United States, or bluntly, why should Americans care what happens in Latin America? (2) Given this importance, are there any adverse trends in Latin America which give cause for serious concern? The next two chapters will consider these crucial problems.

-II-

The Real Importance of Latin America to the United States

In the light of contemporary world power politics, nationalism, and other realities, the United States must continue to base its foreign policy on its own enlightened national interest, must assess realistically its particular interests toward various foreign countries and regions, just as it knows they are doing toward the United States. Such an assessment should be based on the assumption that the United States will be engaged for some years to come in a competitive struggle, increasingly economic and ideological, with the Soviet and Chinese powers; it is true, however, that some of the interests discussed in this chapter would be valid were there no Communist threat at all. Instead of predicating the need for greater attention to Latin America on such high-sounding, altruistic concepts as "good neighborliness" or "humanitarian considerations," let us examine the solid reasons for Latin America's importance to this country. Let us determine why it is vital for our own national interest not only to retain Latin America's friendship but also to advance its welfare. This does not mean that friendly contacts and mutual understanding are not desirable in themselves. Nor does it mean that in the long run, multilateral operations, through the United Nations and other international organizations, should not largely supersede bilateral considerations. But the world is not quite ready for this yet; furthermore the case for increased aid and attention to Latin America can be justified on the ground of national self-interest alone, without reference to any future hypothetical era of mutual world harmony.

One must appreciate the fact that Latin America is now a major region in world affairs and that loss of American prestige there would entail serious adverse consequences for the position of the

17

United States in world affairs. A few neo-isolationists have said that Latin America is the most important area to the United States. This position is as extreme on the one side as is the much more common minimizing of Latin America's significance on the other, and a foreign policy based on it would be inimical to the nation's security. There is enough real substance without exaggerating or distorting the facts.

First it may be well to mention a few considerations that do *not* apply to Latin America. Unlike Western Europe, it does not possess any of the following attributes: sizable, well-equipped, and trained armed forces and armament manufacturing facilities, which could be used immediately to resist a Soviet thrust westward; a large pool of skilled, highly literate manpower with scientific and technical abilities; a high degree of industrialization with a well-integrated steel industry; several world political or economic powers (or even one such power); finally, a strategic location adjoining the Soviet bloc. Southeast Asia, the Near East, and North Africa, though lacking the other attributes, all possess the final one—a strategic location near a center of Communist power. But Latin America has none, which at first glance certainly makes its importance to the United States seem negligible. More careful consideration reveals that at least six features make Latin America very much an area of major interest and concern.

MILITARY SECURITY

Military security is the first and most obvious point. As a glance at the map will show, Mexico, the Caribbean area, and northern South America are a kind of "backyard" with a "rear door" directly into the United States. Furthermore, there are several major American installations of military and strategic importance in the area: not only the Panama Canal, but also the huge Venezuelan petroleum facilities, the refineries on the islands of Aruba and Curaçao, the bauxite resources in Jamaica, and the military bases at Guantánamo in Cuba and in Puerto Rico. It is true that the Canal and the Brazilian hump do not seem as critical now as they once did, in view of new transpolar and other northern bombing

18

routes and modern military strategy in general. Yet the Canal continues to be extremely useful during the present "coexistence" period. Panamanian agitation for greater national control over the Canal, backed up by an Arab-Asian bloc in the United Nations upset over the Suez issue, would certainly be an unpleasant development. As for Venezuelan oil, to the distress of that country and its producers (primarily British and American), it seems to be in excess supply in normal times. But should Near Eastern oil be cut off in an emergency period, this Venezuelan resource would assume quite a different position. The recent Suez Canal crisis and the possible implications of nationalized oil-production facilities in the Near East indicate that further development of Latin American deposits (in Mexico, Peru, and potentially in Brazil and Argentina) should be accorded a higher priority.

The United States could not help but be concerned over any accession to power of a Communist or Communist-dominated regime, or any other kind of anti-American government, in its own backyard. Though it is true that, for logistical reasons alone, the Kremlin seems to have little chance to establish an outright, Chinese-style "People's Republic" in Latin America, the experience in Guatemala is enough to show that one must constantly be on the alert. It does not matter that all the Latin American countries are negligible military powers in terms of modern international warfare. Atom-bombing of American soil from Mexican or Caribbean air bases, or sabotage of the Canal or oil installations, might well occur under deteriorating world conditions. On general principles, these possibilities should never be discounted. Of greater concern is the facility with which saboteurs and enemy agents can slip across the Mexican border (perhaps disguised as "wetbacks") or enter from Cuba.

Finally, there are two ways in which the rapidly growing Latin American manpower pool could be of use in wartime. One is to provide garrisons for Latin American territory and small naval units for coastal patrol; thus the United States would not need to immobilize substantial numbers of its own troops and naval vessels as it did during World War II, especially in Brazil. Secondly, high-quality personnel may be of much greater importance than large numbers of troops during a new war. Several Latin American countries could furnish small yet skilled air-force troops, as Brazil and Mexico did during the last war, as well as perhaps a few atomic scientists and other valuable people.

STRATEGIC MATERIALS

For the United States, Latin America is the source of approximately thirty-five strategic materials, of varying degrees of usefulness. The most important ones are listed below, together with the approximate percentage obtained from Latin America of the total American requirement for each material. A few of these, especially

APPROXIMATE PERCENTAGE OF TOTAL U. S.	
Material	Requirement Obtained from Latin America
Antimony	64
Bauxite	53 (should increase considerably in a few years)
Beryl	49
Copper	27
Iron Ore	7 (estimated to be 10 in a few years)
Lead	31
Manganese	13 (should increase considerably in a few years)
Petroleum	8 (estimated to be 18 by 1975)
Quartz Crystals	92
Tin	17
Tungsten	15
Zinc	18

Chilean copper, Venezuelan petroleum, Brazilian quartz crystals, and Guiana bauxite, have been vital for some time. Brazilian manganese and Jamaican bauxite should shortly enter this category. Many of the others, however, while useful to American peacetime economy, are of critical value only in times of emergency. In some cases, progressive depletion of domestic sources for the raw material makes Latin American sources look increasingly attractive. The best example is iron ore, increasing amounts of which Venezuelan and other sources are now furnishing to the east-coast

20

steel industry. For other materials, Latin American production may be cheaper than domestic, and for still others, notably Bolivian tin, continued high-cost, low-grade production seems important merely because of its more secure location in the Western Hemisphere. A recently published Atomic Energy Commission map showed moderate deposits of fissionable materials in Bolivia, Peru, Chile, and especially Brazil. Though not strategic, coffee and sugar should be included as imports of considerable importance; certain vegetable oils and fibers and medicinal plants also fall into this category.

Constant revision of the entire list is necessary, as some materials increase and others decrease in significance. Latin Americans themselves reportedly are convinced that their many materials have the highest strategic value to the United States. They might be disillusioned by some recent studies which indicate that domestic American synthetics could be substituted for practically all these materials, though often at considerable cost. Another source of worry to Latin Americans is that many of these same strategic materials and others are available to the United States from Asia, Africa, and Canada. Indeed, each of these latter areas can claim that one of its greatest values to the United States lies in its wealth of strategic raw-material resources. As against Asia and Africa, Latin Americans can of course maintain the advantage of having them closer to home.

Surely there is enough reason, then, on grounds of military security and strategic materials alone, to regard Latin America as important. But it would be misleading and unwise to emphasize these easily grasped interests out of proportion to the others. Except in the event of a major war or other emergency, they should not provide the principal balance against which to weigh the Latin American policies of the United States. Many military-minded people seem to feel that as long as the purely military-strategic interests are safeguarded, the United States need not spend much time concerning itself with Latin America. It is our view that to concentrate largely on these aspects is to overlook the more dynamic ways in which Latin America can be helpful in the attainment of

21

American diplomatic, economic, political, and even ideological objectives in the present troubled state of world affairs.

ECONOMIC INTERESTS

The third point of Latin American importance has broader implications than appear at first glance. Americans now have in Latin America a direct and portfolio private investment stake of slightly over $7 billion, which represents about 30 per cent of their total foreign private investment. Even more significantly, about 40 per cent of Americans' total foreign private *direct* investment is located in Latin America, which means that they have larger amounts invested in plants, factories, mines, and other establishments operating in these countries than in any other single area. It is true that the bulk of this investment is in a few countries; Venezuela and Brazil have by far the most, followed by Cuba, Chile, and Mexico. Nevertheless, Americans also have sizable holdings throughout the other nations.

To these large investments should be added a total export-import trade of almost the same magnitude. Latin America, the second biggest foreign customer of the United States, in recent years has absorbed about 20 per cent of its total export trade, mostly in industrial goods, and has supplied a substantially greater portion of American imports, or approximately 40 per cent. Its exports to the United States have been mostly coffee, sugar, oil, copper, bananas, and other raw materials and foodstuffs. Here again one finds a much greater volume of trade with certain countries than with others, but most of those Americans who deal in foreign trade will certainly rate Latin America as a whole among their most important spheres of operations. Not to be overlooked is Latin America's importance to Europe and Japan as a trade partner. It provides those areas with both raw materials and markets for their industries, thereby contributing to the economic strength and stability of the free world.

Thus in terms of private business relations, Latin America rates higher for the United States than any other part of the globe, higher even than Europe or Canada. This has caused most of

22

those who do not put the military-strategic factor in first place to speak of economic relations with Latin America as the one area of importance. Symbolic of this intense economic emphasis is the strong preoccupation in business circles with Latin American affairs, as compared to the relatively minor amount of attention devoted to them in those government or academic circles concerned with global political and cultural relations.

The *amount* of attention paid on economic grounds certainly seems justified, but the *nature* of the emphasis is not. Clearly the material stake held by private American citizens south of the border is a tangible asset that must be safeguarded. When one has several million dollars tied up in a certain Latin American country, one is naturally most concerned with government policies (both American and Latin American) which will affect that capital. Yet it would be unfortunate if a purely material interpretation were placed upon these extensive private business relations with Latin America. For private investment can act as a powerful political and ideological influence by means of which foreign peoples can grow in greater understanding of American ways and methods, and thereby to a pro-Yankee orientation in their general outlook. Enlightened business methods, including government, public, and employee relations, can serve to inculcate habits not only of individual initiative but also of community interest. The same methods can also admirably refute the Communist and ultra-nationalist propaganda, now active in many Latin American countries, which pictures Uncle Sam's big business corporations as purely self-serving and exploitative. In other words, the large economic stake and the principle of enlightened private enterprise are sufficiently important to be safeguarded and reinforced in Latin America.

Nobody who has studied Latin American history will suppose that this can be done easily. The increasing long-range trend is toward a paternalistic nationalism embodying the traditional reliance on central government initiative in economic ventures. The private investor, especially the native one, is still regarded (unfortunately with some justice) as unconcerned with the national

23

welfare. Nor is it here contended that private investment is the panacea for all Latin America's troubles and that governmental and intergovernmental investment should be disregarded. A judicious combination of the two is highly desirable. Greater attention will be given to public and private American economic relations with Latin America in Chapters 6 and 7. Here we wish to emphasize that preserving and increasing a spirit of dynamic, enlightened private enterprise in Latin America can be one of America's greatest accomplishments in world affairs, and thereby a major contribution to its long-range national interest.

POLITICAL SUPPORT

Interestingly enough, when we turn from palpable military, strategic, and economic considerations to the political aspect, we are still on concrete ground. One can easily demonstrate the specific political and diplomatic values to the United States of a favorably disposed Latin America: namely, the twenty Latin American votes in the United Nations General Assembly—one-quarter of the total number of votes in that body—afford substantial support to the United States and its allies, who, in this forum of world opinions, debate many basic issues with the Soviet-Chinese bloc of nations. Latin American support is important, too, in the discussion and resolution of other issues of lesser immediate magnitude but of great long-range importance. The record of United Nations proceedings reveals that on practically all basic issues the majority of the Latin American countries have voted solidly with the United States. In 1952, when the Franco-Tunisian question was under consideration, several carried their support to the point where a majority opposed an Arab-Asian amendment to censure France for its actions. The greater number of the Latin Americans proposed an amendment milder in its comment on French policy; however, it is true that on this issue several Latin American nations—including Argentina, Guatemala, Mexico, Bolivia, and Chile—refused to go along. Similarly, India's attempt, in 1954, to broaden the conference on Korean matters into a general Far Eastern conference, was firmly opposed by the United States,

24

but several Latin American nations did not support the United States.

The split voting on the Tunisian question revealed a Latin American tendency to sympathize with colonial areas, and perhaps a certain susceptibility to Arab approaches for support. Indeed the record shows that on matters important for less developed countries, such as nationalization of resources, several Latin American nations which voted against the United States were sometimes aligned with the Arab-Asian bloc.

So far, such an occasional Latin American alignment with the Arab-Asian bloc has not affected the fundamental balance of power on basic issues. This influential, neutralist "Third Force," however, may well represent another regional bloc, to be added to the Western European Union, the Organization of American States, and of course the Soviet-Chinese blocs. To what extent it will become a really cohesive group remains to be seen. It is possible that the new bloc, which can hardly be termed pro-United States in its orientation, might seek to influence the opinion of the Latin American states and to suggest that they vote more as a *Latin* than as a *Pan* American group—in the spirit of the *americanismo* concept once advanced vigorously by Argentina. Should apathy and neutralism toward "competitive coexistence" increase in Latin America, and attention become concentrated instead on differences between industrialized and less developed countries, an increasing solidarity between the Arab-Asian and Latin groups might well develop.

With the admission of new members, the Arab-Asian bloc had twenty-six members at the end of 1956. Fourteen Latin American votes would assure this group of a majority; only *four* would be needed, if the ten Soviet bloc nations voted with this group. Mexico, Bolivia, Argentina, and one or two others might well defect from the western bloc to give their support to issues such as nationalization of waterways and petroleum facilities.

Some Americans may argue that, in view of Latin America's close economic relationships with the United States, its ability to break away from solidarity with the northern republic on international issues is strictly limited. Such an argument overlooks the growth in investment and trade relationships between Latin American countries and Europe, especially Germany, and also the increasing Soviet bloc trade agreements. While it is true that the economic ties of the Caribbean area most assuredly will remain with the United States, some of the South American countries may move increasingly out of the American orbit.

The fairly consistent Latin American support of the United States in the United Nations exposes these countries to charges of satellitism by the Soviet bloc. Once when the Chilean delegate spoke on the American side of a question, the Soviet delegate launched into a diatribe against domination of Chile by the big American copper companies. He maintained that this made that country in effect a lackey of the United States. More disturbing is the fact that some of America's allies have at times also referred resentfully to the Latin American votes as "satellite" votes, as have certain private American supporters of the United Nations. Presumably these allies would prefer to have the Latin Americans vote against the United States on those issues on which they themselves oppose us.

Of course, the implication in these complaints by friends is that economic, diplomatic, and other kinds of Yankee pressure force the Latin Americans into a bloc vote whenever the United States needs it. Undoubtedly there are considerations of economic aid behind some of the votes—these are the realities of international relations. Nevertheless it seems safe to say that by and large the Latin American nations vote with the United States on basic issues because they believe in its stands on these issues. In view of its general diplomatic neglect of Latin America in recent years, the United States should not be unappreciative of this vital supporting role. Indeed a cynic might well suggest that if any sizable number of Latin Americans were to vote against the United States on some important issues, it might serve to awaken us to the imperative need of paying more careful attention to Latin America!

Support in the United Nations is the most important and easily identifiable political aid that Latin America gives to the United

26

States. There are, however, many instances where friendly Latin American diplomats undoubtedly render informal support to American relations with European, Asian, and Near Eastern countries. In conversations with foreign statesmen and in social contacts with influential citizens of foreign countries, favorably disposed Latin American diplomats can be of great help. A Brazilian friend once pointed out to the author that Brazil, with its substantial number of immigrants from Mediterranean countries, could be of assistance to the United States through its diplomatic and cultural contacts with these countries, implying that Brazilians might have a better understanding than Yankees of Mediterranean culture and way of life. Whether that implication is true or not, such assistance is at least not to be spurned.

With the one exception of the principles involved in economic interests, the points of Latin America's value analyzed thus far have been specific and tangible. The two final considerations, however, belong to the realm of political and ideological estimates, and their implications are more difficult to assess. Yet there is no doubt that these less tangible factors are important to the United States' relations with the rest of the world.

INTERNATIONAL EXAMPLE

The United States, a strong and powerful nation, has been able over a period of many years to develop, in friendly collaboration with its weaker neighbors, a mutually satisfactory system for handling disputes and for protecting one another against outside aggression. Moreover, for two decades this powerful nation has refrained from military intervention in the internal affairs of its neighbors. Obviously frictions and tensions have occurred, and do occur today, but on the whole the inter-American system has worked eminently well. It is in fact the only organization of nations thus far that has been remarkably successful in attaining its objectives. The enduring success of the inter-American system is a notable example to the rest of the world and an outstanding refutation of charges that the United States is an aggressive, imperialistic nation.

27

EDUCATIONAL VALUE

The final consideration, though it really derives from the preceding one, deserves emphasis as a separate and distinct aspect. The success of the inter-American system, particularly in its aspect of nonintervention, has been caused in great part by the ability of the United States to learn how to live peacefully with its often turbulent, and on at least one occasion truly revolutionary, neighbors. This country has learned to exercise self-restraint and only moderate diplomatic pressure in the face of sometimes considerable provocation. These lessons were later of great value when the United States had to deal with Asian and Near Eastern states going through roughly similar evolutions or revolutions. Today, the United States continues to derive valuable experience from its relations with the Latin American countries, many of whom are beset with the same kinds of economic and social stresses and strains that are beginning to afflict several of the Asian countries. Thus, Latin America has a constant educational value.

The enumeration of the ways in which Latin America is important is based on present and probable near-future conditions. It does not take into consideration the possible introduction of a radical new factor into the industrializing economies of at least the major Latin American countries—atomic energy. Were this to happen during the next decade or two on any significant scale, Latin America would assume a more important role in world affairs than it does today. It would begin to be prized as a valuable industrial complex, as Western Europe is now. The twenty votes in the United Nations would come from nations with a greater economic impact on the world and their growing segment of the world's opinion would count for more. Prospects for such an atomic transformation do not seem bright in the short run. It may well be, however, that in the not too distant future certain nations, especially Brazil, will be able to use their atomic materials to build atomic energy plants, thus avoiding to some degree the great expense of electric power installations.

Certainly it seems clear that the United States should take the lead in helping Latin America develop its atomic energy, thereby retaining its enlightened leadership of the Western Hemisphere. At the same time it would gain experience in utilization of this peacetime energy of the future. At the 1956 inter-American presidential meeting in Panama, the United States appeared to take the first steps toward such a forward-looking policy.

In at least six ways, then, Latin America is important to the United States. It has, of course, many other values and attractions, such as a humanistic culture, leisurely pace of life, and racial attitudes, all deserving close study (and perhaps some imitation) by Yankees, and its pleasurable vacation attractions always beckon. But our paramount consideration here is with those matters specifically concerned with United States foreign policy.

It seems clear that if Latin America were to become alienated from the United States, if anti-Yankee sentiment were to increase strongly throughout Latin America, and if ultranationalists and Communists were correspondingly to enlarge their influence and strength, the United States might well find itself confronted by a hostile or at least a neutral Latin America. Such a state of affairs would mean that the vital importance which Latin America now holds would to a considerable degree be nullified. Though not critically threatened, the United States could no longer feel militarily secure and might have difficulty in obtaining the strategic materials it needs. American business enterprises in Latin America would certainly encounter growing harassment, and our neighbors would probably make efforts to increase their trade with Europe and the Soviet-Chinese bloc at American expense. The blocs would, for political reasons, doubtless make even more attractive trade bids than they offer presently. Good will toward the United States would tend to evaporate, many of the twenty United Nations votes would be aligned against this country, the inter-American system would encounter increasing obstacles. Probably the hostile activities of most Latin American countries would eventually have a limit, in view of the considerable economic dependence upon the United States, but not before the situation had worsened.

At this stage, an interesting paradox is already apparent. On

29

the one hand, the manifold importance of Latin America to the United States and the unhappy consequences of deterioration in present relations have been stressed. On the other hand, conventional images of Latin America certainly encourage Americans to take it for granted. What is the rationale for this paradox? It would appear that most of the factors of importance are not dramatic ones, largely because of Latin America's geographical remoteness from the centers of present-day world power. Nor are these factors of the type to stimulate the thoughts and lives of many United States citizens. It might be wise, therefore, to consider especially those factors which are not so impersonal or immutable as military security or strategic materials, but which offer dynamic possibilities for capturing the imagination.

Only one seems to have these qualities, namely the economic factor. The possibilities inherent in an intensive inter-American effort to utilize the hemisphere's substantial economic potentialities appeal to both the businessman and the average American citizen. Developing an iron-ore deposit or a large chemical works through a combined-capital venture, using a World Bank or Export-Import Bank loan to build a power plant or a railway, establishing a Point Four project with Latins and Yankees working together— these can entice the imagination and at the same time are concrete. In the next decade, the economic impact of Latin America will continue to be of prime importance. The twenty United Nations votes in the next few years depend to a considerable degree, though by no means entirely, on this cementing of stronger economic bonds. Then, with expanded two-way trade reaching many private citizens, both south and north, and with the eventual completion of the Pan-American Highway and increased air-travel facilities, the cultural interaction between the two parts of the hemisphere will undoubtedly become steadily more intense. In other words, if the economic trend which takes place is a mutually beneficial one, a "meeting of the minds" should be greatly facilitated.

Let us now consider the second question raised at the end of Chapter 1: Are any adverse trends evident in contemporary Latin America that give the United States cause for serious concern?

-III-

Trends of Concern: Dictatorship, Nationalism, and Communism

Today a good part of Latin America is at last undergoing a fundamental transformation, which the United States, in the light of recent Asian experiences, must watch carefully for trends that might be adverse to its interests. This change perhaps is best dramatized by contrasting the amusing stereotype of the sleepy Mexican peasant and the grim picture of the peasant-worker revolutionary guards in the National Palace in La Paz, Bolivia. The sleepy peon, the lazy urban worker are no longer indifferent; they are restlessly seeking the better things of life so long denied them. Improving health, literacy, transportation, and communications are at last endowing these people with the possibility of improving their lot, if they are ably led. Unfortunately, as we shall see, movements embodying their hopes have sometimes been captured by strong-armed leaders, and the people have bartered what political and civil freedom they had (admittedly little in some cases) for social progress. Regardless of how it is channeled or manipulated, this so-called "revolution of rising expectations" is on the move today throughout most of Latin America, nor is it surprising to find that it has become intertwined with two contemporary great political movements, nationalism and Communism. Let us examine, first, the trend toward dictatorship in Latin America, not to pass judgment on it as a form of government, but to determine whether it possesses an actual or potential threat to the best interests of the United States and the inter-American community.

Until around 1930 in most Latin American countries, traditional conservatives and liberals had alternated in control of their governments. When they were other than purely personalistic, such labels were meaningful only in terms of procedural political differ-

31

ences; namely, strong executive versus weak, centralization versus regional autonomy, and established Church versus separation of Church and State. Alternating, largely upper-class, political regimes governed a semifeudal, latifundiary economic and social order.

In view of the frequently adverse comments in recent years concerning the appearance of numerous repressive Latin American dictatorships, it is well to keep in mind this oligarchical tradition. For hundreds of years, in colonial times as well as during independence, most parts of Latin America have known nothing but authoritarian rule, at its worst tyrannically repressive, at its best benevolently paternalistic. Democracy, as we know it in the United States, was not totally absent in the southern lands, but it seemed to be the exception. The authoritarianism inherent in traditional institutions such as the army, the family, the church, the state, or the school has tended to breed acceptance of authoritarian controls generally. This acceptance may well continue for some time to come, notwithstanding the impact of new political pressures from organized labor, middle-income groups, and other elements. Indeed, within these groups the old authoritarian habits may well prevail to a considerable degree, reinforcing dictatorial patterns and largely preventing the growth of a democratic orientation. The simplest and most graphic way of emphasizing this point is to say that as long as the army remains the principal instrument of power in Latin America, authoritarian rule will probably prevail. This is especially true as long as control of the governmental bureaucratic machinery also gives control of the lucrative sources of income from tax revenues and foreign concessions.

Therefore, dictatorship is not a new nor even a recent phenomenon in Latin America. True, in the nineteenth and early twentieth centuries, Argentina had a long period of relative democratic government, and in this century Uruguay, Chile, Costa Rica, and until a few years ago Colombia were ruled by generally democratic regimes. Brazil and Ecuador in recent times have had periods of democratic experience. These are exceptions to the rule, however. Even in Mexico, which is sometimes referred to paradoxically as a "one-party democracy," and in which a violent change in the relative positions of the social classes took place, the president in effect still rules paternalistically. True, the various new social sectors— agrarian, labor, and middle-class—are provided with flexible and changing participation in the government via contested "primaries." And opposition to the ruling party is gradually gaining headway over the years. But it has not yet won any really significant number of votes in the elections, and one party continues to have completely decisive control over matters.

If, then, authoritarian controls are generally traditional in most Latin American countries, why not simply accept them as a normal and natural pattern? Why should the United States concern itself over the rash of dictatorships appearing in the last few years? Have they not brought political stability and economic progress to many of these nations? Certainly Americans should at all costs avoid the mistake of condemning foreign regimes simply because they do not happen to be similar to the United States' form of government. There may be many humanistic values, at least in the more benevolent paternalisms, which, unlike totalitarian regimes, leave religion, family, and in general the "way of life" relatively untouched. The dictatorship in Bolivia has been simply one illustration of this.

There is nevertheless a reason for concern over the new type of dictatorship that has appeared in some countries. The general political trends in these dictatorships have been roughly parallel in such significant Latin American countries as Argentina, Peru, Venezuela, and Colombia. Admittedly there were greater complexities in the Argentina case, yet the resemblances to the other countries were also striking. The pattern in the "one-man rules" in the Dominican Republic, Nicaragua, and the other small, less developed countries has not thus far been so complex, perhaps largely because of the almost complete lack of any real middle groups in the population. But with future economic development these countries too may follow roughly parallel political routes. It should also be made clear that *long-term* trends are being considered here. A democratic turn might seem to have taken place in 1956 in Peru, but underlying power factors are largely similar.

The modern-style dictatorships received their original impetus around 1930 with the combination of the depression, Italian Fascist and corporative influences, and Communist appeals. Small, elite groups of politicos, army officers, schoolteachers, and intellectuals (plus for the first time a handful of labor leaders) were either in exile or prison, or at least strongly out of sympathy with the existing incompetent, oligarchical regimes. The violent attainment of power by the exiled groups delivered the *coup de grâce* to the old liberal-conservative alignments. As state planning for elaborate economic and social objectives took place, practically for the first time in most countries, liberals and conservatives split into conflicting wings. The liberals found themselves torn between the desire for freedom from central control and the wish to bring about social progress and economic equity through government planning. The conservatives found themselves torn between the desire for a centralized, paternalistic government and a disinclination to legislate reform for the lower classes.

With the possible exception of Argentina (and even there it is doubtful), these countries have never had a well-established, economically independent and secure middle class, with a strong sense of political consciousness and active participation in representative government. Instead, the middle-income groups were on the whole politically fragmented and disoriented. Meanwhile, people from the countryside came to industrial opportunities in the urban areas and swelled the ranks of city workers and lower-income groups in general. The conservative and liberal upper classes and fragmented middle class were thus confronted by newly swollen cities with lagging basic facilities, new lower-income groups, labor unions growing in political power, higher costs of living, and in most cases traditionally inefficient and corrupt governments.

The new urban laborers, often uprooted from their stable clan-*patrón*-godfather relationships, were faced with the impersonality and restless dissatisfaction of the cities and with contrasting, often juxtaposed, wealth and squalor. Consciously or unconsciously, they were searching for a new and broader framework of social relations to take the place of the old emotional props and provide

34

comradeship and solidarity. At the same time, the laborers were vulnerable to nationalistic and extremist appeals. This was most evident in Colombia, where they found a rabble-rouser in Jorge Gaitán, whose assassination precipitated the Bogotá riots, the famous *bogotazo*. Even rural labor began to stir, but so far it has not been well organized; the determining factors in the national political leadership continue to be urban. This general phenomenon invites comparison with the appeals made to new urban workers by illegal trade unions and certain popular leaders in "underdeveloped," mid-nineteenth-century England.

Obviously great strains and pressures ensue in such a situation. The conservatives offered no program to cope with the changing social situation, and the liberals, split into left and right wings, were unable to unite on constructive measures or even to maintain themselves in office. Labor unions, governmental creations in any case (except in pre-Perón Argentina), were increasingly inclined to look up to the "democratic Caesar," the new *patrón* who would assure both a strong and stable government and gains for labor. Conservative, high-ranking military officers assumed dictatorial control, although the initial strong man in Colombia, Laureano Gómez, was a civilian. The result was that the labor unions were completely "captured" by the new authoritarian regimes which, it must be admitted, gave them at least in the short run substantial economic and social advantages. The regimes did this, partly to entrench themselves more firmly in power as the incarnation of the "popular will," but also for nationalistic reasons to increase the productivity of the workers and thereby further industrialization.

In none of the countries has there been a one-man dictatorship, an unassailable *El Supremo;* instead a military-civilian junta has shared the power, to which the term "creole fascism" has sometimes been applied. The "cult of Bolívar" in the Andean countries, which stresses the Liberator's emphasis—in the latter part of his career—on a strong executive, seems to be a rationalization for absolute power.

A careful appraisal reveals that these dictatorships were able to gain control not so much by their own repressive strength as by default. Only in Peru was there a long-standing dynamic movement led by the Apristas under Haya de la Torre. However, this group, bitterly opposed by the armed forces, seemed to lose its capacity to mobilize public sentiment and to translate its ideas into forceful and yet practical initiative. In all the countries, the longer the dictatorships continued, the more they became a vested interest; with press censorship, the increasing corruption was concealed from the public. In Venezuela, election results which were proceeding unfavorably to the regime in power were falsified to show victory, and later election day was celebrated as a national holiday! Meanwhile, democratically oriented labor unions have been suppressed. Opposition groups in exile or in prison have become increasingly disunited and embittered, often turning their resentment against the United States, which they excoriate for "propping up" dictatorship and "Fascism" in our hemisphere. One needs only to glance at some of the letters to the *New York Times* from Latin American exiles in the last few years. Some of these people, though not pro-Communist to begin with, have become willing at last to join forces with the Communists in order to return to power. Naturally too, the dictatorship will take advantage of any opportunity for referring to the opposition as "Communists." Those opposition groups which have remained at home have grown ineffective and often apathetic; indeed, the longer the opposition has been out of power, the more it has lost touch with the increasingly complex problems of governing a modernizing country.

Thus it becomes clear that what is to be condemned by thoughtful Americans is not authoritarian rule in Latin America per se. Rather, it is the consequences enumerated above that may ensue from the contemporary dictatorships which are to be considered adverse to the interests of the United States. One might almost say that the problem does not rest in the traditional paternalistic pattern itself, but rather in the distortion of that pattern which has been forced by the incapacity of the old traditional regimes to meet the complex needs of the modern era. The inefficiency that seems to be an inseparable characteristic of the old-line authoritarianism does not provide enough grounds for condemnation of the system,

36

but unfortunately it has in some cases created frustrations that extremist forces have exploited. Most important of the "isms" that have fed on the stresses and strains are, as might be expected, nationalism and Communism. (It should be made clear that these forces are to be found in varying degrees in all Latin American countries, not just in the dictatorships.) Let us examine first nationalism, the primary force.

It is intriguing to speculate at exactly what points in their histories Latin American countries began to be conscious of the fact that they were "underdeveloped" and became imbued with a desire for national economic development and social and cultural progress. Again, for many nations, the year 1930 may be regarded as a catalytic one for the same general reasons as those that gave rise to the modern-style dictatorships; at that time, too, the depression sharply focused the economic issues by wreaking havoc with Latin America's vital foreign trade. Nationalistic urges multiplied with the advent of World War II: the need for industrialization became acute and foreign-exchange balances, with which sizable amounts of capital goods could at last be obtained, steadily increased. It must not be forgotten that the United States greatly stimulated this urge for national development, by continually reiterating to Brazil and other "retarded" countries, that they should make every effort to modernize and industrialize. In one sense, then, nationalism in Latin America may be viewed as simply the most sharply expressed political reaction to industrialization's impact on primarily agrarian economies.

After the war many of the republics in which nationalism was burgeoning expended large percentages of their exchange balances on luxuries rather than on capital-goods imports (for example, Brazil) and soon found, to their misfortune, that their plans for industrialization were largely frustrated. No Marshall Plan aid was forthcoming; World Bank and Export-Import Bank loans seemed both excessively delayed and inadequate. A sizable amount of American private investment was flowing in, but this gave rise to politically inconvenient charges of foreign exploitation. Meanwhile, pressures continued from most of the population for social

37

development and progress, neither of which could be put off indefinitely.

Yet frustrations have continued to ensue from the inability of Latin American leaders to achieve this progress. A few have candidly acknowledged that this failure comes in great measure from the difficulties of adapting anachronistic administrative structures and social and cultural institutions to modern industrial needs. Many other leaders have chosen the path of political expediency by attributing their shortcomings to a scapegoat. The United States has seemed the most likely candidate for this position, for in the eyes of many Latin Americans it has in the postwar years neglected to extend sufficient economic aid to its southern neighbors, and at the same time has continued to take advantage of them through its large business interests and controls over raw-material prices.

Many historians will argue that Latin American nationalism is not a recent phenomenon. They will find evidence of it even in pre-independence days and certainly throughout the nineteenth century and early years of this century. For instance: Does the expressed desire of some statesmen in mid-nineteenth-century Brazil to operate their own railway system indicate growing nationalism at that early date? In the early years of this century were the violent outbursts of resentment against Yankee interventions in the Caribbean area, which appeared in Nicaragua, Haiti, the Dominican Republic, and Colombia, examples of nationalism? Finally, what about the intense feeling in the 1920's, shared by Haya de la Torre's handful of Peruvian intellectuals, against the oppression of Yankee imperialism? The following comments are ventured: all these manifestations were negative, that is, they were directed against alleged foreign exploitation. Xenophobia had come down from colonial times when upper-class Spanish American *criollos* felt they were being discriminated against and exploited by the Spanish *gachupines*. It had continued in the minds of at least some thoughtful and sensitive people throughout the nineteenth century, when it was directed increasingly toward the large British, and later American, economic influences over their countries. On the other hand, one must remember that many of the leaders, particularly the *caudillo* dictators, were perfectly happy to obtain loans and do other business with foreigners, and that most people were too preoccupied with eking out a bare existence to think much about foreign domination.

The contention here, then, is that modern nationalism did not become pronounced in Latin America (except in Mexico) until the 1930's. By modern Latin American nationalism, we mean the affirmative, vigorous expression, by influential opinion-molders, of a country's national character and interests, and concrete actions to advance those interests, often against foreign influences. Such a nationalism is almost invariably accompanied by considerable analysis of the past shortcomings of the country and its people (a kind of inferiority complex), and speculation as to what the "genuine" expression of the nation's "personality" should be; both of these characteristics are revealed in the works of Brazilian essayists in the 1930's. Usually a major effort is made to nationalize the public utilities, railroads, important industries, and mines, to praise the national product, and to rewrite the constitutions in order to emphasize national economic controls, political and social order, and the dignity and rights of national labor. Active xenophobia chooses as its main targets Yankee business interests, and by extension economic imperialism, partly because Americans are the primary foreign investors and partly because the United States is the richest and most powerful nation.

It is to be noted that Latin American nationalism differs from the ex-colonial Asian brand in that it has primarily an economic emphasis rather than a political one; however, both reveal strong sensitivity to domination (whether political or economic) by foreigners. Naturally there are varying degrees of nationalism in Latin America, but it appears to be on the increase everywhere.

Now it seems pointless to condemn this nationalistic trend. Notwithstanding complaints by advocates of world government, nationalism still appears to be the major force in the modern world, as nations like India, Egypt, Indonesia, and Israel can well testify. Some people escape this dilemma by approving nationalism but condemning so-called ultranationalism, which of course begs the question of where one ends and the other begins. It might be said that ultranationalism, at least in Latin America, begins when the attempts to encourage national pride and free the country from hampering foreign control over its economic life reach the point of an insular negativism that blindly rejects everything not purely national in origin. The most frequently cited example is Brazil's prohibition against significant foreign participation in the vitally needed development of its petroleum resources.

Clearly much more study must be devoted to the rise, present state, and probable future trend of nationalism in Latin America. Thus far this nationalism has appeared to be primarily economic, usually directed against Yankee business concerns and the competition of foreign professionals, and such a direction obviously threatens United States foreign-policy objectives. How much of Latin American nationalism is artificially fostered by the governments and vested private interests and how much is the expression of a genuinely conscious (or even "subconscious") national sentiment must be determined.

One thing certainly seems clear: the anti-United States sentiment and the as yet unrealized desires for economic and social progress, born of nationalism, have been grist to the Communist mill. The Communists, of course, have not caused but have only stimulated the nationalistic feelings of outside exploitation; that is, the primary force in contemporary Latin America (just as apparently in non-Communist Asia) is nationalism. Yet Communism nevertheless is a force to be reckoned with in Latin America today, for it can exploit both the increasing nationalistic feelings and the repressive features of the modern dictatorships.

The dictator himself sometimes finds it expedient to enter into a temporary partnership with the Communists, knowing that they are generally disliked and that they can be repressed at any time without arousing major antagonism. Meanwhile the Communists, long used to persecution, play this cynical game of power politics and bide their time, often suffering together with genuine liberals under a totalitarian regime. Then, when the regime topples, as it must eventually, the Communists are in a strategic position to enhance substantially their influence. If and when they do gain strength and influence, it is primarily because other movements have failed to provide dynamic initiative, either through constructive opposition to a dictatorship or by enlightened leadership in a more democratically oriented country undergoing the severe pains of industrial growth (for example, Brazil). To blame the economic and social problems on exploitation by American business interests is obviously an adroit tactic here. How much headway have the Communists been able to make by taking advantage of the above conditions?

Fortunately, an official report by the United States Senate Special Subcommittee on Security Affairs of May, 1954, contains a brief but careful analysis of this subject and appears to reflect the situation generally as it was through 1956. The membership figures (always of course an estimate) indicated that from a total of around 330,000 in 1944-1947, Communist *card-bearing* membership has dropped to about 200,000. In the majority of the countries, the party is officially suppressed. It has no present prospect of gaining control over any Latin American government by electoral means. Nor does it have any significant direct participation in national politics since the failure of its effort in Guatemala.

These data must, however, be weighed carefully. The decline in the total number probably means only that many of the "fringe" members and sympathizers have dropped out, leaving plenty of hard-core, disciplined members to cause trouble. In countries with a small minority of educated people and only a few strategic labor unions, a few well-placed Communists can be very effective, as the Guatemalan situation showed. Official suppression of the party has comparatively little effect on its political and ideological influence, as Brazil and Chile demonstrate.

The subcommittee's report points out that there may be a million or more latent sympathizers throughout Latin America. It warns that Communists occupy a number of key positions in strategic labor unions and federations, educational systems, intellectual circles, and patriotic and ultranationalist organizations. The short-run objective of the Communists is to locate political power in

41

the hands of groups hostile to the United States and thus neu-
tralize Latin America as an effective ally of the United States.
On this basis, they will generally support a group of any political
persuasion, so long as it is anti-Yankee. The United States is pictured by Communist propaganda as an exploiting, warmongering
power, and an offensive is carried on against United States-Latin
American military assistance agreements and the participation of
American capital in the development of raw-material resources.
The contemporary trend is to form "national liberation fronts" with
patriotic groups, to fight for national independence, social justice,
economic democracy, and labor unity. Particular target groups are
organized urban labor, intellectuals, women, and youth.

Though the present Communist situation certainly does not leave
one complacent, neither should it be taken to mean that Communism
is today a critical or immediate threat in Latin America. Only in
Guatemala did the Communists achieve maximum gains. It is
extremely difficult to evaluate real Communist strength and influence in any Latin American country, because of the volatility of
the political and emotional environment and the difficulty of
estimating how effective the army and conservative-moderate groups
would be in checking Communist moves in time of crisis.

Communists today would appear to have their greatest potentialities in Brazil and Chile. Though the Senate report gave 60,000
(in a population of about 57 million) as the estimated membership
of the illegal Brazilian party, subsequent press reports indicate that
there may be about twice as many. If true, this would make the
party in Brazil the largest outside the Iron Curtain, except for
those in France and Italy. Again the significance of mere quantity
is problematic, but even if they are not highly effective, 100,000
Communists in this key country cannot simply be shrugged off.
They publish more newspapers than any other single political
party: a fact not to be taken lightly. Chile, with a reported 40,000
illegal Communists for only 6 million people, has the greatest
number per capita. They are said to have control of some fairly
high-ranking positions in the member federations of the National
Labor Confederation (CUTCH). Some sources state that, since

42

1949, Chilean Communists have lost much of their influence, but their great strike potential makes them an important force to contend with. As we shall emphasize later, even weak Bolivia, with its tiny and fortunately divided Communist movement, can never be ignored.

The Kremlin has made considerable efforts to increase Communist strength and influence in Latin America. Though exact statistics are naturally impossible to come by, information drawn from official publications and informal estimates reveals that in 1953 and 1954 a thousand Communists and sympathizers were invited to visit the Soviet-Chinese bloc, twice as great a number as were invited in 1952, and ten times as great as in 1950. Latin Americans who visit behind the Iron Curtain are undoubtedly royally treated and their personal roles as reformers and "progressives" in "underdeveloped" countries similar to the bloc nations are duly appreciated. Some may be impressed with the applicability of the "Yenan Way" of Maoism to the agricultural countries of Latin America. The expanding Soviet trade missions to, and agreements with, Latin American countries cannot help having a psychological impact. Moscow also transmits broadcasts in Spanish and Portuguese to Latin America, but their impact is difficult to judge. The fact that the Soviet-Chinese bloc has no direct involvement, and thus cause for friction, with Latin America gives it certain advantages over the United States in this use of psychological warfare.

The role of the Roman Catholic Church as a force against Communism generally has not been too strong. Probably the explanation lies in the Church's present-day paucity of material resources (as compared to its former opulence in many countries like Mexico), the shortage of qualified priests to service large territories, its unfortunate lack of interest in social progress, and finally the fact that many Latin American leaders and men of action are only nominal Catholics. A few encouraging signs, however, such as the recent Catholic agrarian conferences in Colombia and Panama and the activities of priests in Argentine labor unions, indicate that the Church may be more of a force in the future. The Church is reluctant to become actively involved in politics, in view of its former experiences with conservative-liberal battles and the turmoil incident to the Mexican Revolution, but it could certainly be a spiritual or ideological weapon against Communist beliefs.

4 Thus the old order changeth in Latin America. Unfortunately many Latin American leaders and political thinkers are not fully aware of this economic and social transformation, not only the conservative landowners but even many liberal intellectuals. Because of their default and the ensuing political instability, a modern brand of dictator has stepped in to direct the destinies of the state and restore a dubious order and stability. Meanwhile the opposition forces—who, though not completely democratic, at least offer some support for human and civil rights—have fallen out of touch with the complexities of modern government. They have become increasingly embittered or apathetic and strongly critical of the United States; and therefore increasingly susceptible to the appeals of Communism. The new nationalism, with its emphasis on pride in things national, and on an economic trans- formation with the controls in national hands, has impregnated both the ruling groups and the opposition.

The Communists take advantage of both the nationalism and the dictatorial suppression to further their own power objectives. In particular they seem anxious to win over young people, who are more malleable, and women, who may influence both the children and sometimes their husbands (for example, Señora Arbenz in Guatemala). Thus an increasing number of the new gen- eration in Latin America may become influenced by Communist ideas. Labor leaders and intellectuals are particular targets in this Communist battle for men's minds. The Soviet bloc's guided tours behind the Iron Curtain certainly will favorably impress many of these people, particularly since they can see clearly the pro- nounced inequities and general retardation of their own societies. All this does not mean that Communism will become in the imme- diate future a critical threat in Latin America, though the move- ments in countries like Brazil and Chile need particularly careful scrutiny.

Let us now turn to the part that the United States itself has

44

played, and may play in the future, in influencing the course of developments in Latin America. The role of the United States may be considered to have three general aspects—political, economic, and ideological. Under the political category, two basic problems have loomed prominently throughout the years: (1) how to avoid Yankee intervention in the internal affairs of the weak Latin American countries; and (2) how to make the hemisphere secure against aggression, both from within and from without, and more recently from the new kind of internal subversion by international Communism. To put these problems somewhat differently: How can the United States utilize her military and economic power to protect the Western Hemisphere, without in the process meddling in the internal affairs of the Latin American countries? Let us discuss first the general problem of intervention and its reverse, nonintervention, which has been of the greatest concern to Latin Americans.

-IV-

Defining Yankee Intervention

At first glance what people think about past inter-American relations seems to be more important than what actually happened. Years may be spent digging up documents about past Yankee military and political actions in Caribbean countries, yet the common view that the United States was aggressively imperialistic, that its large corporations were deliberately exploiting the southern lands, is altered not a whit. That many Latin Americans (and some Yankees) have continued to feel aggrieved by past American policies is understandable: anyone carefully and honestly weighing the available facts cannot but conclude that Yankee actions in Panama and the Caribbean area during 1900 to 1930 fitted under one of the several definitions of "imperialism."

It is of more interest to note that this characterization of the United States seems to have become part of our national heritage. Many American historians and writers have accepted the epithet uncritically, particularly during the Good Neighbor and World War II periods (1938-1944), when a plethora of books about Latin America, many of them superficial, came tumbling off the presses. Only one writer, a distinguished diplomatic historian, was an exception; he presented a strong strategic case for "protective" imperialism. More recently, scholars have made more searching judgments of American policies, but "imperialism" continues to be the accepted term.

Were this now a purely academic subject, it would not be significant in a foreign-policy discussion. Unfortunately, throughout the world imperialism has become, without much Communist urging, the usual description of past American policies in the Western Hemisphere. The Guatemalan episode in 1954 tended to reinvigorate such thinking. Moreover, Indian intellectuals are said to believe that, beginning at the turn of the century, the United States changed from an unaggressive into an imperialistic nation. Now there is no intention here to prove that past actions of the United States could not be characterized as "imperialistic," nor to whitewash specific episodes. Instead we should like to focus on the highlights of the past as a testing ground where the United States has been learning by trial and error how better to formulate and implement its Latin American policies.

The first focal point is certainly the Monroe Doctrine. By means of this doctrine, the United States with the aid of the British navy and some later unilateral Yankee interpretations, was able to keep European interlopers out of the Western Hemisphere. For a number of years the doctrine was either passively accepted or largely ignored by our southern neighbors. Later, as their fear of European intervention ebbed, they became increasingly hostile toward the disposition of the United States to interpret the doctrine as a means for advancement of what they considered Yankee rather than Latin American interests. Understandably they did not feel that the interests of the United States were necessarily "those of civilization." After years of poor relations between the United States and the increasingly stronger Latin American countries, the doctrine at last became inter-American in its lineaments. Thus the Monroe Doctrine in its pristine form became outmoded; it is still valid, but has been adapted to New World conditions and international concepts. Yet there is a tendency in some quarters to overlook the earlier usefulness of the doctrine, to regard it either with hostility, as a cloak under which Yankee imperialism could extend its sway over certain parts of Latin America, or with distaste as an anachronism. Thus, historical policies of the greatest constructive significance often need periodic reinterpretation. Even this will not prevent their use by some as a means of constructing a history of unpleasant inter-American relations.

Consider another famous episode in inter-American relations, the Panama incident of 1903. This seems to be the only incident concerning which all agree, north and south, that the United States committed a clearly identified injustice against a Latin American country. It is true that later research showed that Colombia stalled for a considerable length of time in order to get better financial terms for the Canal concession, and that it knew that there might well be serious trouble on the part of the Panamanians, should negotiations with the United States not be completed. But there is no doubt that our government was guilty of connivance with the Panamanian revolt, by preventing the Colombians from landing troops and by recognizing quickly the independence of Panama. Unfortunately it took a distressing nineteen years to effect a final settlement of this incident between the United States and Colombia; first Colombia refused to be reconciled in 1909, and later certain elements in our government delayed resolution.

Latin pride was hurt here, and American political leaders revealed their own haughtiness too. To lose a good part of one's territory is indeed a humiliating experience, as Mexico could testify from her nineteenth-century history. Yet not a single Colombian was killed as a result of the incident; the Canal has been a great boon to Colombia, to Latin America, and to civilization as a whole. No Yankee forces occupied Colombia's main territory in South America. By comparison the countries in the Caribbean area which were the scenes of outright Yankee occupations would seem to have a stronger case for long-enduring resentment. In all fairness, today most Colombians admit the great value of the Canal and, while naturally not excusing American conduct, they no longer harbor intense grudges against the United States because of it. Nevertheless, beginning with the fiery poems of the Nicaraguan poet, Rubén Darío, against Theodore Roosevelt ("the eagle with a thousand claws"), the Panama incident has been for many years one of the chief weapons in the armory of Latin American anti-Yankeeism. But in the light of events and injustices of the last two decades throughout the world, which make Yankee behavior in Panama pale into insignificance, is not half a century long enough to apologize?

Let us turn next to another often-cited historical basis for anti-Yankeeism, the landing of marines, seizure of customs revenues, and other domineering actions in Cuba and other Caribbean countries in the years 1900-1933. It would be oversimplification to postulate only one motive for these actions. Undoubtedly military and strategic considerations played their part. The most obvious one was a well-grounded concern that deterioration of law and order and inability to pay European creditors might lead either to European intervention or to some other situation adverse to American interests. Creating political conditions more favorable to American business interests seemed at times to be a factor, especially in Nicaragua. And let us not overlook missionary and humanitarian impulses to spread some of the benefits of a "superior" civilization to "backward" southern neighbors, to build schools and hospitals, and to eradicate certain diseases. It is essential to note that United States forces eventually withdrew from all these countries and that this kind of intervention has not been repeated. Thus Theodore Roosevelt's so-called "Big Stick" or "policing" corollary to the Monroe Doctrine had various facets, though many refuse to explore them and are content merely to label the United States "aggressively imperialistic."

American policy-makers did learn some valuable lessons from these episodes. They learned that there was not much use in attempting to dictate the choices of political regimes, either by "landing the marines" or by employing recognition of the regimes as a persuasive weapon. They might be able to cause a regime to topple by not recognizing it, but the regime they preferred, perhaps more favorably disposed toward business interests, would become the target of Yankeephobia and lose its internal support. They also learned that a policy of vacillation aroused just as much criticism as did repression. To intervene in Cuba on earlier occasions, but not to do so during the brutal, increasingly unpopular Machado dictatorship, confused and embittered many Latin Americans, and was not consistent with the best American interests. The policy of interference also vacillated in Nicaragua. There acts of repression led to the rise of a guerrilla patriot and intense popular hostility. This pattern was repeated in Haiti and the Dominican Republic.

It was, however, different and perhaps irrelevant for the United States to ascertain the attitudes of the "people" of these countries.

49

Social stratification and the concentration of political power were so pronounced that an oligarchy controlled all important activities, and offered the only significant opinion. Some of these ruling elements wanted American troops in the country, often to strengthen their own position against the opposition. For example, Rafael Trujillo used his position as chief of the American-fostered *gendarmerie* to gain undisputed possession of the Dominican Republic. Whether the occupations were for or against the best interests of the mass of the people generally did not seem to matter much to either the Latins or Yankees.

Still another lesson was that the many material benefits—reduction of debts, improvements in governmental administration, construction of schools, hospitals, and roads—all laudable in themselves, did little to stimulate the growth of political democracy. This will be seen later to have some application to present-day economic aid and the Point Four program.

The interventions in the Caribbean area tagged Americans as imperialists more than any other phase of their Latin American policies. They caused a wave of Yankeephobia to sweep over Latin America, culminating in the Pan-American Conference in 1928 at Havana. One could not entirely escape the impression that some of this hostility was fomented by Argentina, in its pursuit of an oppositionist *americanismo* policy of solidarity for Latin Americans, but there was no question that spontaneous anti-Yankeeism was rampant. In the face of this feeling, attempts to explain the bases for Yankee conduct met with little sympathy. The following words of Secretary Charles Evans Hughes at Havana made a favorable impression on the United States Chamber of Commerce, but certainly not on most Latin delegates:

We would leave Haiti at any time that we had reasonable expectations of stability. . . . We are at this moment in Nicaragua; but what we are doing there and the commitments we have made are at the request of both parties and in the interest of peace and order and a fair election. We have no desire to stay. We entered to meet an imperative but temporary exigency; and we shall return as soon as possible.

Nor did the efforts of the American delegation at the Conference meetings to distinguish between temporary "interposition" and permanent "intervention" meet with approval.

Another clear and impressive lesson to American policy-makers, which came from the early Mexican experience (1912-1917), was the failure of a new kind of intervention, now characterized by historians as "moral imperialism." President Woodrow Wilson made strong efforts to unseat the "bad" Huertista government and to put into power a "good" one, chiefly through the weapon of diplomatic recognition. This ethnocentric attempt to impose one's own criterion of good government merely made the "bad" regime stronger, by stirring up Mexican nationalism and resentment at Yankee meddling. Later the lesson had to be learned all over again with Spruille Braden and Perón in Argentina.

By 1930, it had become clear that in the interests of hemispheric amity, the United States had better agree that it would never again intervene in the international affairs of its neighbors. In that year, J. Reuben Clark prepared a memorandum on the Monroe Doctrine which was published as an official document by the Department of State. It declared Roosevelt's "Big Stick" corollary to be unjustified by the terms of the Doctrine. The publication of this memorandum assured Latin America that the United States would definitely desist from its former activities. The way was thus paved for the Good Neighbor Policy of President Franklin D. Roosevelt.

In 1933, at the Inter-American Conference at Montevideo, the United States among other things accepted, with reservations subject to international law, a convention wherein it was agreed that "no state has the right to intervene in the international or external affairs of another." In 1936, at the Inter-American Conference at Buenos Aires, the United States ratified this nonintervention protocol without reservations. According to the protocol, the internal affairs of any of the parties did not admit of intervention by any one of them, and violations should give rise to mutual consultation. In the next few years the principle of nonintervention was honored by the United States during the dispute of Lázaro Cárdenas' Mexican government with the foreign petroleum companies. In 1945, a Uruguayan proposal was made to provide for *collective* intervention in any country where human rights were severely transgressed. This was understood generally to be directed against the neighboring Argentine regime, and it had informal Yankee backing. It failed to receive any support, however, from the rest of the inter-American community. The non-intervention principle was confirmed at the conference in 1945 at Mexico City; at Bogotá in 1948 it was written into the OAS charter (Article 16).

On none of these occasions was an attempt made to define *precisely* what constituted intervention in the internal affairs of a country. Probably in those days the delegates had in mind no other action than the traditional "landing of the marines," that is, military interposition, and possibly the use of diplomatic nonrecognition as a weapon.

For the United States to contravene the sacred precept of non-intervention would be not merely to violate an inter-American agreement that it has willingly signed, but also to open up an old sore, aggravate anti-Yankee feeling, and give the Communists a valuable propaganda asset. The matter thus seems at first glance to be definitely resolved. But the world today is in a situation quite different from that of two decades ago. There are two major alterations in the international scene as far as Latin America is concerned. First, international Communism in postwar years has been far more capable of penetrating Latin America. This implies that special measures, both policing and economic-social, must be adopted to make this hemisphere impregnable against the blandishments of Communism. Second, irrespective of Communism, the Latin American countries look increasingly to the United States to help them achieve rapid economic progress. They now want Yankees to be not just "good neighbors" but also "good partners." How, then, can the United States achieve these objectives without breaking its nonintervention pledge?

One quick way of disposing of this problem would be to let responsible Latin American opinion itself judge whether any given move of the United States in Latin America constitutes intervention in internal affairs. But American foreign-policy officials will certainly want to have clear in their own minds what is meant by intervention.

Certain types of actions can hardly be characterized in any other way than as flagrant intervention. They are military occupation, severance of diplomatic relations, nonrecognition of a government, organized economic boycott, and, especially in the instance of a small country, direct interference by a large American business concern in internal politics. The last type is not, of course, *official* intervention, but in the minds of people in the country involved it is tantamount to it. These practices of the past are what most fair-minded people mean by intervention. There are other types of deliberate Yankee actions, however, which may intentionally have an impact on the internal course of events in a country. For example, what about economic aid that directly affects the political situation in a country, as in Bolivia and Guatemala? How about a speech by an American ambassador either praising or criticizing the regime of the country where he is located? There are several other kinds of interaction, some more subtle but nonetheless significant, which we shall explore shortly.

Meanwhile, in order to avoid constant confusion in terms, let us attempt a working definition of Yankee intervention in Latin America. It is *direct interposition by the United States alone of military force, or diplomatic or economic sanctions, in any Latin American country.* It would still be intervention, even if the action took place upon the request of, or with the acquiescence of, the ruling faction or any large segment of the people in the country. All other kinds of actions, however decisive or influential they may be, are not to be considered intervention. These other actions can be called "interaction" or "mediating by persuasion and influence." This relatively clear distinction provides a guidepost for foreign-policy decisions regarding Latin America. We are quite willing to admit that, to be realistic, the kinds of action lumped under "interaction" and "influence" could be labeled a sort of intervention. What really counts here is not niceties of international law, but

53

whether any sizable segment of responsible Latin American opinion feels that internal Latin affairs have been interfered with. In any case, if we adopted such a broad definition of intervention, practically every foreign-policy move undertaken, even inaction such as not granting a loan, would have to be considered intervention! This does seem to be carrying things too far.

Before proceeding to discuss the various kinds of actions which the United States might take without intervening, we should not omit from brief consideration one type of extreme situation. Given the realities of military and political power today, unilateral Yankee intervention might have to take place to meet a critical threat to United States security. In this case, however, there would be no doubt that the nonintervention principle would thereby be violated, and the advantage gained in resolving the crisis quickly would have to be balanced against the severe, perhaps permanent damage done to inter-American relations. The Guatemalan case, to be analyzed later, was closest to this kind of emergency situation. Obviously unilateral measures should be eschewed unless the point of desperation were reached. The United States should furnish ample information to the Latin American nations concerning any serious deterioration in security and consult with them well beforehand about appropriate action. This would be in keeping with both the letter and the spirit of previous inter-American treaties and agreements. After all, a community of mutual interests does exist, and actions undertaken by the United States are not designed to advance its own selfish interests exclusively, but also the interests of the whole Western Hemisphere.

What, then, are some of the many kinds of interaction and "mediating influence" which the United States might take without being accused by Latin Americans of intervention? They can be grouped under various headings—economic, diplomatic, political, and ideological. In the Bolivian and Guatemalan cases, economic aid to tottering regimes probably saved them from quick downfall. In Bolivia the United States threw its economic weight behind genuine indigenous reformers, in order to avert chaos and extremism. After having been forced into negative "firemen's tactics" in Guatemala, the United States finally adopted affirmative economic measures to help a regime, which though unfortunately not so progressive as the Bolivian, nevertheless was (through 1956) the best alternative available. In Brazil, there is no immediate danger of economic or political collapse, but continued rapid economic growth is essential to stability and progress. Furthermore, friendly Brazil has long been the key ally of the United States in Latin America and must be kept strong. Large-scale American loans have been necessary and will continue to be so in the future to prevent a deterioration adverse to both American and hemispheric interests.

Another kind of economic interaction is the purchase of particular raw-material exports at stabilized prices, a practice usually helpful in warding off political instability in certain countries. In recent years exports that have given trouble have been Bolivian tin and Chilean copper. Venezuelan oil, and Brazilian, Colombian, and Central American coffee may be added to this list in the future. Private American concerns operating in Latin America can have an important direct economic impact by renegotiating contracts, such as those signed by the United Fruit Company with Guatemala and Costa Rica. Also of great importance is the entrance of new American capital.

The American ambassador in a Latin American country can hardly avoid the strong use of diplomatic influence. In 1936 Secretary Cordell Hull sent the following instructions to our Central American missions: "The Ministers should abstain from offering advice on any domestic question, and if requested to give such advice they should decline to do so." This stricture may have been wise at that time, but today it is doubtful if most missions can feasibly follow it. The late Ambassador John E. Peurifoy's key intermediary role in Guatemala's violent change of regime was the most striking instance of the vital part which an official American representative can sometimes play. In many Latin American countries, particularly the smaller ones in the Caribbean area, the American ambassador exercises, by virtue of his office, a great influence. The local authorities will often seek his advice, and though sometimes he may feel that he is not in a position to give it, in other

55

cases it may be wise to do so. Occasionally, he might on instructions from Washington find it necessary to give unsolicited advice concerning a delicate domestic situation. For example, suppose that Communists or other anti-American individuals were lodged in the foreign office or in a government propaganda agency, where they were responsible for the adoption of certain anti-American policies. The ambassador might wish to bring this situation to the attention of the foreign minister, pointing out its detrimental effect on relations between the two countries, with the obvious implication that the offending individuals be removed from their key posts. This is certainly an example of strong diplomatic representation, and also underscores the importance of good personal relations between the American ambassador and the high government officials of the country concerned, particularly in personalistic Latin America. Diplomatic representatives should be experienced in the peculiar volatility of the Latin American atmosphere.

Politically, influence can be exerted in various ways, some of them indirect but nonetheless effective. A speech by an ambassador or a State Department official, praising the development of democracy by a certain Latin American regime, may cause "strong man" regimes to wonder if allowance of more freedom in their countries might not raise their prestige in Washington's eyes. For example, former Assistant Secretary Edward Miller in an official speech referred to Chile as having the kind of democratic government that the United States liked to see in Latin America. Statements by private American organizations, particularly powerful business and labor groups, can help to encourage those who are struggling to maintain democratic government in Latin America. An excellent example is this statement by the American Federation of Labor, praising the steps taken by the Organization of American States to restore peace in the Figueres-Somoza dispute:

The A.F.L. strongly urges our Government to spare neither effort nor energy nor resources in enabling the progressive Republic of Costa Rica, where the free trade unions are a bulwark of its dynamic democracy and determined opposition to Communism and all other forms of dictatorship, to beat back all aggression.

Another political move, this time a negative warning, was the dispatching of American planes to Panama and Central America as a thinly veiled hint to Somoza not to abet aggression of Costa Rica.

These and other actions with political overtones may help further democratic government in Latin America. So also may certain ideological gestures; for example, endorsement of a resolution on human rights at an inter-American conference. Indeed, whenever possible the United States should reaffirm its underlying belief in democracy, liberalism, and morality. To cynics, such gestures might seem empty platitudes, but they are meaningful and pertinent to those Latin Americans struggling against the heritage of centuries to bring about democratic government in their countries. Ideological influence can also be exerted within a dictatorship by the program of the United States Information Agency (USIA), which by showing the way of life in American democracy may encourage democratic thought in the country's inhabitants. Within limits these actions with political and ideological overtones can be highly fruitful.

Here we come to what is probably the most controversial contemporary Latin American subject for both the northern and southern citizens of the hemisphere. Given its nonintervention pledge, what policy should the United States adopt toward repressive dictatorships? Opinion is sharply divided on this matter. American liberals condemn the dictatorships and, urged on by Latin American exiles, complain that the United States is shamefully supporting them. Mindful of the Braden fiasco, few liberals would now demand that the United States openly attempt to unseat the dictators, yet they feel that nothing should be done to aid them in any way. But such a course would include prohibition on loans, and perhaps even on Point Four assistance, as well as diplomatic and political aloofness. One sympathizes with the long-range goals of the liberals, but is their policy really feasible? In the first place, the United States would have to "cold-shoulder" at the present time at least half a dozen Latin American countries including, to be consistent, the enlightened dictatorship in Bolivia. Or should one differentiate among the dictatorships, sitting in judgment on each?

It is our view that as long as a dictatorship is anti-Communist and is not openly anti-Yankee, the United States should neither favor it nor discriminate against it. *This does not constitute approval, but rather formal adjustment to a reality.* True, a point might be reached where the regime, even though it passed the above tests, might be so brutally callous of human rights that to continue relations with it would sorely try the American conscience. Did the Perón regime reach this point? Has Pérez Jiménez or Trujillo? It is difficult to pass moral judgment on these matters. Let us emphasize once again that dictatorships are traditional in many Latin American countries, largely because of the authoritarianism, or at least paternalism, inherent in the general structures of their societies. Americans should not expect other countries to have our particular type of democratic structure. Some of the exiled liberals, when in power, have revealed themselves to be authoritarian in their approach. And a good many of the exiles, despite their support of the nonintervention principle, would like to have the United States meddle in their countries' internal affairs, to the extent of getting them back into power. One need hardly ask how this kind of intervention would affect American relations with Latin America in general.

Should Americans, then, shrug off dictatorships in Latin America as inevitable? The answer is no; there should be an underlying moral consensus of aversion to dictatorial repression of human rights, and a corresponding general affirmation of belief in democracy. Certainly no unusually warm *abrazos* nor special honors need be accorded dictators. On the other hand, it might be well to commend authoritarian regimes when they do undertake some genuinely constructive measures, instead of concentrating on adverse criticisms. Enlightened elements have existed in the national heritage of most Latin American countries. The United States, by appealing to national pride in these aspects of their history, rather than by setting itself up as an example, might accomplish more. In some cases, the accomplishment may not be great, and certainly will not seem so to frustrated and bitter exiles, but Americans are formulating a foreign policy for their own country, not for the interests of exiles.

A final plea is in order to those Americans who criticize openly relations with the dictatorships. They should at the same time express an appreciation of the dilemma involved. It is easy to decry the present situation; it is far more difficult to suggest any feasible alternative. Some measures can be taken to further the growth of democracy in Latin America, but they are limited in scope and must be oriented with great care so as to avoid the charge of Yankee intervention. Latin America is progressing, rapidly in some areas, but political and social evolution has its unpredictable aspects, and one should not expect Latin America necessarily to evolve into the American type of government and society. Particularly when one reflects upon the use to which Communists and other anti-Americans around the world put these adverse criticisms, Americans should at least make sure that their criticisms are well pondered and responsible.

-V-

Hemispheric Security

Though our Western Hemisphere community is primarily concerned with its general welfare, it should not neglect the policing aspect. Certain groups may attempt to attack or subvert a particular country, as in Guatemala or Nicaragua and Costa Rica. Inter-American facilities and procedures must be available to investigate and handle expeditiously these threats to the peace. Sometimes force, or implied force, must be a necessary instrument of foreign policy. In the Latin American area it is essential that these instruments be wielded on a multilateral rather than a unilateral basis.

There are four principal ways in which the security of the hemisphere might be threatened: (1) extra-hemispheric attack by one or more powers; (2) aggression toward one Western Hemisphere state by another; (3) subversion of a country by Communist or other infiltration from within or without the hemisphere; (4) a revolt clandestinely assisted, but *not officially* supported, by one hemispheric state against another. Other, imaginable circumstances could result in lesser threats. For example, the perennial boundary disputes between certain countries, notably Peru and Ecuador, have sometimes flared up to the point where outside conciliation and arbitration have been necessary.

Until 1947, measures to safeguard against external aggression were emphasized, though during World War II some attention was paid to Axis subversive activities. Since then, however, main concerns have been the combatting of Communist infiltration and subversion and protection of small Latin American countries from revolts launched from outside their borders. Because of their clandestine nature, these newer threats to hemispheric security have proved more difficult to cope with. Doubt has been expressed

60

as to whether the existing treaty provisions for hemispheric security are adequate for the contemporary era. In order to understand these provisions, it is well to trace their evolution.

In the years leading up to World War II, the United States was anxious to build up a system of consultation among the hemispheric states that would lead to unanimous action in the event of extra-hemispheric aggression. Thus, the Monroe Doctrine, by which the United States had unilaterally protected the Western Hemisphere, would be multilateralized. With the exception of Argentina, the Latin American states were favorably disposed toward this move, but as we have seen, their principal concern was to commit the United States to an international guarantee that it would not intervene by force in their countries. They also wished to outlaw wars of aggression and compel the settlement of disputes by legal means, and to this the United States agreed.

Though some preliminary steps had been taken at earlier inter-American conferences, the first real attempt to coordinate and strengthen the inter-American peace machinery occurred in 1933 at Montevideo. Various arbitration and conciliation treaties existed, but needed coordination and amalgamation, and several countries had not even ratified them. With the senseless Chaco War between Bolivia and Paraguay serving as a tragic warning, the statesmen at Montevideo, led by Argentina's Saavedra Lamas, outlawed wars of aggression and made an effort to establish a standard procedure for settlement of disputes by legal means. The Hoover-Stimson doctrine of nonrecognition of territorial changes brought about by force was recognized as satisfactory, and the signatory powers agreed to sanction political, judicial, and economic means, "but in no case shall they resort to intervention, diplomatic or armed," to solve problems.

Further codification and coordination of the various inter-American instruments to deal with maintenance of the peace, antiwar declarations, and forcible acquisition of territory were achieved in 1936 at Buenos Aires. It was agreed that, should the peace of a hemispheric republic be threatened by any source either at home or abroad, consultation should be held immediately with a view to cooperative action to preserve the peace. But the American proposal, that a permanent body consisting of the foreign ministers of all the states should carry out the provisions, failed. The republics also repeated earlier obligations and pledges and provided for individual or joint offers of good offices or mediation. The signatory powers agreed that upon the threat of war, the parties concerned should delay six months for consultation before initiating hostilities; they further agreed that, if war did break out, they should adopt a common attitude of neutrality, and, in order to prevent the spread of hostilities, should impose restrictions on sale or shipment of munitions and on financial assistance to the belligerents.

The over-all objective during this period was clearly to assure the maintenance of peace through mutual consultation and cooperative action. Yet the general impression is that the Latin American states primarily wished to protect themselves from military or diplomatic intervention by the "Colossus of the North," rather than from an outside power, or from one another. Also, Argentina, notwithstanding its championship of general principles of international law, had shown itself reluctant to establish a really effective system for carrying out the desired consultations regarding threats to the peace.

At Lima, in 1938, Secretary Hull was able to obtain the unanimous action against the threat of autocratic aggression that he had long sought. First, the principle of continental solidarity and the decision to defend it against all foreign intervention were reaffirmed. Next, a definite procedure of consultation in the event of emergency was established. If the peace, security, or territorial integrity of any hemispheric republic should be threatened, consultations would be held by meetings of the ministers of foreign affiairs, when it seemed desirable and was initiated by any one of them. Many other principles were agreed upon, later known as the "Declaration of Lima." The most important of these were proscription of the use of force as an instrument of national or international policy and revision of treaties by peaceful methods only.

62

The provision for emergency meetings of foreign ministers was made just in time. From 1939 to 1942, with the Axis threatening the hemisphere, three such meetings had to be held. Most of the matters discussed were relevant to the wartime emergencies only, but three measures were of lasting significance in the postwar period. One was the Act of Havana, in 1940, which declared that any state in an emergency might act singly or jointly with others in its own defense, or in defense of the continent. This act was to lay the basis for the right of immediate self-defense while waiting for the consultative machinery to swing into action. The other two measures were adopted in 1942 at Rio de Janeiro. At that meeting an Inter-American Joint Defense Board, still active today, was created to study and recommend measures for defense of the hemisphere, and an Emergency Advisory Committee for Political Defense was established to suppress Axis subversion in the hemisphere. The organizational and procedural methods of this committee supplied a precedent for coping with the struggle against international Communist activities. At the inter-American meeting in 1945 at Mexico City, the Inter-American Joint Defense Board was made permanent, and cooperation against subversive Axis propaganda was strengthened.

At this meeting, the inter-American system faced the first great postwar challenge to its very existence. The United States, preoccupied with setting up a strong United Nations, was concerned lest regional agreements interfere with it. On the other hand, the Latin American states wanted to preserve a strong regional agreement against aggression. A compromise, known as the Act of Chapultepec, was reached, whereby a postwar treaty was to be signed that would strengthen the inter-American security system, but adhering to the principles and purposes of the new international organization. This treaty was to embody the following principles: in the case of aggression against a hemispheric state, whether from without or within the hemisphere, the signatory countries should consult as to action. Aggression was defined as armed trespass and various counteractions might be employed, including severance of diplomatic relations, imposition of an economic boycott, and

63

use of armed force. At the meeting a resolution was passed to hold meetings of foreign ministers annually and inter-American conferences every four years. Broader powers were given to the representatives in the Pan American Union.

The historic Inter-American Treaty of Reciprocal Assistance was signed on September 1, 1947, at a foreign-ministers' meeting in Rio de Janeiro. In effect, it made permanent the stipulations of the Act of Chapultepec as to mutual assistance, and improved the machinery for administering this assistance. Since the treaty is the basic instrument for defense of the Western Hemisphere today, let us consider the articles of major importance:

1. *Article I*—The High Contracting Parties "condemn war and undertake in their international relations not to resort to the threat of use of force in any manner inconsistent with . . . the Charter of the United Nations or of this Treaty."

2. *Article II*—High Contracting Parties will undertake to submit every controversy arising between them to peaceful settlement through procedures of the Inter-American System before referring to the General Assembly or Security Council.

3. *Article III* (in case of attack from within the Western Hemisphere, including Canada and Greenland)—"The High Contracting Parties agree that an armed attack by any state against an American State shall be considered as an attack against all the American States, and consequently, each one of the Contracting Parties undertakes to assist in meeting the attack in the exercise . . . of individual or collective self defense recognized by Article 51" of the United Nations Charter.

Until the meeting of the Organ of Consultation of the Inter-American System, each State or States may determine the immediate measures to be taken in fulfillment of provisions above. The Organ of Consultation shall determine the collective measures.

4. *Article VI* (when an attack against a State or States is made from without the Western Hemisphere)—If the integrity or sovereignty or political independence of an American State should be affected by other than armed aggression or by extra-continental aggression and thereby endanger the peace of America, the Organ

of Consultation shall meet immediately to agree on measures to be taken in case of aggression.

5. *Article VIII*—The measures which the Organ of Consultation may determine to take are:

(a) recall of chiefs of diplomatic missions
(b) breaking off of diplomatic relations
(c) breaking off of consular relations
(d) partial or complete interruption of economic relations
(e) use of armed force.

Thus the republics of the Americas had agreed unanimously that an attack upon one is an attack upon all. When the attack is internal, immediate and effective action is promised; when it is external, immediate consultation looking toward united action is guaranteed. Despite Argentina's efforts to require unanimity in calling for a meeting of the Organ of Consultation (foreign ministers)—in effect allowing a veto power—a two-thirds vote was deemed sufficient. Also defeated was an Argentine attempt to make the treaty inapplicable in the case of attack against American forces stationed abroad. The United Nations references in the first three articles showed the consistency of the inter-American statesmen in adhering to the principles and procedures approved by that organization, as agreed upon in Mexico City in 1945. Later, the Guatemalan case emphasized that the drafters of the United Nations charter had left a certain undefined area of responsibility between the United Nations and the inter-American regional organization. The Rio Treaty (as it is generally called) served as a predecessor to the North Atlantic Treaty Organization (NATO). It has never been invoked, although its tenets were reflected in the anti-Communist declaration in 1954 at Caracas.

A further step toward improvement of the mechanism for inter-American defense was taken in 1948 at the Inter-American Conference at Bogotá. At this meeting it was decided that the Inter-American System should be called the Organization of American States, that conferences should be held every five years, and that consultation meetings of foreign ministers should be convoked when needed. The signatory powers obligated themselves to settle all

65

disputes by such peaceful means as good offices, mediation, and arbitration.

In 1947, however, even before the Rio defense treaty was signed, an historic turning-point occurred in American foreign policy that confirmed the United States' diversion of attention away from the hemispheric security system—a diversion that had already taken place during World War II. On March 12 President Truman in effect made explicit and formal the departure of the United States from hemispheric isolationism. The seizures of Hungary and Czechoslovakia plainly indicated that the aggressive expansion of the Soviet Union and international Communism would have to be contained. The president stated that the United States would have to defend itself at a great distance, rather than on its own beaches. He said that it must be the "policy of the United States to support free peoples resisting attempted subjugation . . . " and expressed the "frank recognition that totalitarian regimes imposed on free peoples . . . undermine the foundations of international peace and hence the security of the United States." In retrospect, one is tempted to criticize the president for not having substituted the words "Western Hemisphere" for "United States." One might also wonder why he did not consult the foreign ministers of the southern republics before making this important pronouncement. It must be remembered, however, that Congress had first to approve his policy; furthermore, it is doubtful whether the Latin American countries would have been willing to extend their interests outside of this hemisphere.

Since 1947, United States foreign policy has been chiefly concerned with the anti-Communist struggle. Consequently, emphasis has been placed on the Truman Doctrine in Greece, NATO, Southeast Asia Treaty Organization (SEATO), and other defense organizations and measures involving areas far removed from hemispheric shores. Even the Marshall Plan and, to a considerable extent, Point Four technical assistance have been conceived of in anti-Communist, "defense in depth" terms. Little attention has been paid to the Rio treaty mechanism.

In 1951, when the United Nations took action in Korea (with

the support of Latin American delegates), there did seem to be an occasion to activate the inter-American security system. At a meeting of the foreign ministers in Washington, the Inter-American Joint Defense Board was strengthened, and an increase in the production of Latin American strategic raw materials and the dispatch of troops was requested. However, Korea was geographically remote, the stepped-up supply of certain materials produced an embarrassing surplus later, and only Colombia sent any troops.

Practically the sole security concern within the hemisphere since 1947 has been the struggle against infiltration and subversive activities of international Communism. Latin Americans, however, have not been nearly so perturbed as Americans with this overriding objective, and have maintained that the best way to combat the growth of Communism in Latin America is to facilitate economic and social progress. Notwithstanding this view, they have been willing to adopt a series of resolutions condemning international Communism as a menace and suggesting certain specific measures to combat it.

The first of these resolutions, passed in 1948 at the conference at Bogotá, declared that "by its anti-democratic character and interventionist tendency, the political activity of international communism or any totalitarian doctrine is incompatible with the concept of American freedom. . . . " This resolution was a step forward, but it considered Communism only as another totalitarianism; furthermore it provided no procedures to be taken if the threat materialized. The Rio treaty, of course, stated the course of action in the event of internal or external aggression against the hemisphere, but the vague wording of the Bogotá resolution made it impossible or at least extremely difficult to apply the Rio treaty measures against Communism. An effort to bridge this gap at least partially was made at the 1951 meeting in Washington, with this addition:

It is in accordance with the high common and individual interests of the American Republics to meet the special and immediate threat of subversive action of international Communism. Since the said subversive action recognizes no boundaries, the present

67

situation requires adequate internal measures, and a high degree of international cooperation looking to eradication of any threat of subversive activity which may endanger democracy and a free way of life in the American Republics.

Since this statement was still vague, it was hoped that at the Inter-American Conference at Caracas, in March, 1954, a much more definitive step forward would be taken, particularly in view of the Guatemalan situation. What issued from that conference, called the "Declaration of Solidarity for the Preservation of the Political Integrity of the American States Against the Intervention of International Communism," represented only a slight advance. In effect, it applied the provision against aggression in the Rio treaty to that part of the Monroe Doctrine warning against the extension of an alien political system to this hemisphere. The declaration states:

. . . The domination or control of the political institutions of any American State by the international communist movement, extending to this Hemisphere the political system of an extra-continental power, would constitute a threat to the sovereignty and political independence of the American States, endangering the peace of America, and would call for a Meeting of Consultation to consider the adoption of appropriate action in accordance with existing treaties.

The declaration also called upon each American state to adopt internal measures against Communist activities and to exchange information concerning them with other countries. How fruitful this part of the resolution will prove remains to be seen. Guatemala was not mentioned, because to single out one country would have weakened the long-range value of the declaration. Argentina and Mexico abstained from voting in favor of this declaration, and some of the others voted only reluctantly, since they feared it might lead to intervention.

The United States clearly would have liked the inter-American community to have adopted more specific measures against the extension of Communism, particularly with reference to Guatemala.

Three months later, the shipment of Iron Curtain arms to Guatemala awoke the Latin American states to the real danger. The anti-Communist revolt obviated the necessity of holding another meeting, but the Guatemalan case flung at the OAS its first big postwar challenge and raised fundamental questions as to the relationships between the OAS and the United Nations.

In the account that follows, the dilemma of the United States will become somewhat clearer if one understands that the Arbenz regime in Guatemala had fallen under the influence of Communists to the point where it was in effect a puppet of the Soviet Union. Obviously the United States would not be at all unhappy to see the regime topple and an anti-Communist one take its place. The other non-Communist nations represented on the United Nations Security Council frankly were little concerned about Guatemala itself or the tradition and prestige of the OAS; their main objective was to safeguard the broad jurisdictional authority of the Security Council.

The Arbenz government, on June 19, 1954, cabled both the Inter-American Peace Commission (IAPC) of the OAS and the Security Council, requesting aid as a victim of "aggression" by Honduras and Nicaragua, instigated by certain "foreign monopolies" that were against the "progressive" policies of the Guatemalan government. On June 21 the government withdrew its request from the IAPC and left the matter exclusively to the Security Council. For on June 20 the council, though referring the matter to the OAS despite a Soviet veto, had passed a French proposal calling for an immediate termination of hostilities which might cause bloodshed. Thus, while the Arbenz regime had originally placed its case before as many peace enforcement groups as possible, it had now apparently decided that it preferred to have the broader, international group handle it exclusively, in particular one on which the Soviet Union was represented.

The attitude of the United States government was that Guatemala was not the victim of aggression, but rather that this was a "revolt of Guatemalans against the Government." In the time-honored Latin American sense, it was a "revolution" or "civil war" and

69

belonged clearly to OAS regional jurisdiction. But, Henry Cabot Lodge, Jr., then president of the Security Council, explained in calling a meeting that

the United States believes in the basic proposition that any member, large or small, has the right to an urgent meeting of the Security Council whenever it feels itself to be in danger . . . even when, as is sometimes the case, the Security Council may not itself be in the best position to deal directly with the situation.

At the Security Council meeting, Lodge declared that the Soviet veto could not fail "to make unbiased observers throughout the world come to the conclusion that the Soviet Union had designs on the American hemisphere" and warned the Russian delegate to "stay out of this hemisphere and do not try to start your plans and conspiracies over here." Tsarapkin, the Russian delegate, replied that the case was one of aggression, in which "a Member of the United Nations has been subjected to an armed attack provoked, organized, and carried out by the United States of America."

After such exchanges it was no wonder that Lodge felt that another meeting on the subject would be unproductive. When Guatemala soon afterwards alleged that the cease-fire had not been obeyed and requested another meeting, Lodge stated that "a meeting had been held and that there seemed to be no point in holding another." As president of the council, however, he felt constrained to grant a second hearing, which took place on June 25. The only item was to decide whether the Guatemalan case should come up for discussion again. A motion to that effect failed to carry, but France and Britain abstained, and Denmark, Lebanon, and New Zealand voted against the United States.

The United States had therefore achieved its objectives of warding off Soviet meddling in the affairs of the Western Hemisphere, and placing jurisdiction over the matter in the hands of the OAS, where it rightfully belonged. Yet many nations which usually voted on basic issues with the United States felt that in this case it was wrong that any nation in the world, particularly a small one, should have the right at least to be heard by the Security Council whenever it desired. The non-Communist delegates believed the council should have allowed discussion of the Guatemalan case for the second time and then voted again to refer it to the OAS. To deny the right of a small nation to be heard was setting a dangerous precedent, as Lodge himself had remarked not long before in connection with the Thailand case. Nobody had questioned Guatemala's *right* in the first place to notify the Security Council concerning its trouble and to request its aid, since appropriate articles of the United Nations Charter could be found to substantiate this action. The question was whether the council was obliged to handle the case, or merely should decide whether it should handle it.

Though the United Nations Charter does not give a clear-cut answer, it would seem to suggest the second course of action. Article 52 states that "members of the United Nations . . . shall make every effort to achieve pacific settlement of local disputes through such regional agencies *before* referring them to the Security Council." It also declares that "The Security Council shall encourage the development of pacific settlement of local disputes through such regional arrangements or by such regional agencies either on the initiative of the states concerned or by reference from the Security Council." Article 37 states that should parties to a dispute endangering the maintenance of peace fail to settle it in some other way, including via regional agencies, they should refer it to the Security Council.

These articles certainly give priority to regional action. Moreover, at both the Inter-American Conference at Mexico City in 1945 and the meeting to formulate the United Nations Charter in San Francisco later in the same year, the Latin American nations (including the liberal Arévalo regime in Guatemala) had determined that the United Nations should supplement—neither substitute for nor impair—their own regional agreements. Thus, the Latin American community seemed unanimously to favor OAS jurisdiction over inter-American troubles, and indeed even appeared to feel more strongly about this than the United States. After all,

71

if the OAS was not allowed to handle the Guatemalan case, what real purpose did its existence serve? Here was a golden opportunity for it to handle its first really major controversial problem and thereby raise its influence and prestige in the eyes of the whole world.

Nevertheless, there were some inconsistencies. For example, in the case of Korea, the United States had argued that an invasion of their own country by nationals backed with international Communist aid was clearly aggression, but in Guatemala anti-Communist nationals invading their country were engaged in an internal "revolution" or "civil war." Regardless of the niceties of international law, there is no need for the United States to apologize for making this distinction, in the light of political realities. Yet it did confuse some people. In particular, it led President Somoza of Nicaragua to believe that he could assist with impunity an invasion from his territory of Costa Rica, instigated and carried out by Costa Rican non-Communist nationals. Because this dispute illustrates, like the Guatemalan one, a complex problem for the guarantors of hemispheric security, it is well to examine it more closely.

José Figueres, president of democratic Costa Rica, had long had a personal feud with Anastasio Somoza, president of the neighboring Nicaraguan dictatorship. This animosity was based partly on purely personal antagonism, and partly on genuine ideological differences. Figueres averred that he symbolized the democratic hopes of Latin America arrayed against Somoza's "strong-man" type of caudillo-dictatorship. Somoza in turn regarded the Costa Rican leader as an unstable, leftist liberal who was setting a bad example for other Latin American regimes. Furthermore, strongman Somoza, Pérez Jiménez of Venezuela, and Rafael Trujillo of the Dominican Republic had long harbored grudges against Figueres because he offered Costa Rica as a safe haven and a center of political intrigue for exiles from their regimes. Somoza and Figueres each accused the other of being a party to hostile actions against the other.

In the spring of 1954, an unsuccessful attempt to assassinate Somoza was made by a group of oppositionist conservatives, who crossed the Costa Rican frontier into Nicaragua. Naturally Somoza accused Figueres of complicity in the plot. Though Figueres personally was not involved, he probably knew that the scheme was being hatched on his territory by the conspirators. Particularly damaging was the fact that he happened to be near the Nicaraguan border at the time of the attempt.

The next move was Somoza's. In July, 1954, the dictator deployed some of his troops along the border of Costa Rica in a show of armed strength. It is now clear in retrospect that, at least from this time on, he must also have materially aided Costa Rican exiles who were preparing, on his territory, for an invasion of Costa Rica. From November 20 on, there were persistent rumors that an uprising would take place.

During this period, officials in Washington were not ignorant of what was going on. Indeed they engaged in tactics that might be described as "psychological warfare," clearly designed to warn Somoza. On the occasion of his show of armed force in July, the United States Air Force sent six jet planes on a "good-will" visit to Costa Rica. In August the United States sold a half-million dollars' worth of rifles, machine guns, and mortars to Costa Rica. Carried out under the standard arrangement of a Mutual Defense Assistance Pact, the sale enabled Costa Rica to replenish the worn-out equipment of its Civil Guard. Costa Rica's generally pacific attitude appeared in the lengthy debate over acceptance of the offer, on the grounds that it would violate the country's nonmilitary tradition. Actually the arms were to prove vital in repelling the rebel invasion. The next American warning to Somoza in the period before the invasion was another dispatch of six planes to Panama, at the time of the rumored uprising in November. The meaning of these gestures was clear, not only to Somoza but also to the rest of sensitive Central America. It would appear, however, that Somoza apparently decided in the next few months that though it would be most unwise for Nicaraguan forces openly to invade Costa Rica, a clandestinely assisted revolt by Costa Rican exiles, in the Guatemalan style, could be carried off without serious outside interference.

Thus, on January 10, 1955, a group of not more than a thousand Costa Rican rebels, well armed with mortars, machine guns, and a handful of planes, invaded Costa Rica from Nicaraguan soil. They were headed by Teodoro Picado, Jr., a 1951 graduate of West Point, and son of a former president whom Figueres had defeated in 1948. Later it was discovered that these rebels had trained on Somoza's personal estates and were furnished air support from Nicaraguan bases. The rebels obviously hoped that, with their modern equipment, they could overcome the supposedly weak resistance of Costa Rican forces and occupy the capital, San José, before the OAS could intervene. The OAS (and the United States) would then be presented with a *fait accompli,* as it was in Guatemala.

With the Guatemalan precedent obviously fresh in their minds, the rebels charged that Communists held influential positions in the Figueres regime and called upon the Costa Ricans to flock to their banners. Somoza declared that the rebels would lay down their arms if the Costa Rican government would guarantee them amnesty and free elections—an interesting statement to come from a ruler who had not allowed free elections in eighteen years! Volunteers in most parts of Costa Rica sprang to the defense of their country. Costa Rican home forces quickly mobilized sizable contingents, superior in morale, and probably about equal in equipment, to the invaders. Their one great disadvantage lay in the total lack of an air force, in comparison to the small one in possession of the rebels. Here the OAS, in addition to its broader moral and political suasion, was to provide concrete help.

On January 8, 1955, Costa Rica had warned the OAS that a rebellion against it was developing in Nicaragua, and that it might soon have to ask for help—a request that came on January 10. The OAS decided to postpone its meeting until January 12; during this time much thought was given by the various nations as to the jurisdictional approach. Was this a matter for the Inter-American Peace Commission to resolve, or was the Nicaraguan government actually participating in an invasion of another Latin American country, in which case a meeting of inter-American foreign ministers should be held? At the meeting on January 12, it was decided to send the IAPC investigating team to study the situation, and since the team named no official aggressor, the IAPC was given jurisdiction over the conflict.

The investigating team, headed by Dr. Luis Quintanilla of Mexico, was composed of one representative each from Mexico, Brazil, Paraguay, Ecuador, and the United States (Ambassador John C. Dreier). In view of an impudent "buzzing" by a rebel plane, the team accepted an offer by the United States navy or armed observation planes from the Canal Zone. Within twenty-four hours, the investigating group discovered that a substantial amount of material had been introduced over the Costa Rican border from Nicaragua. Therefore, a request by the Costa Rican government for planes was granted on January 15; an American offer of four fighter planes at a token price was accepted; the planes arrived on January 17; and three days later flights began.

The investigators carefully avoided all contact with the rebel forces, and no territory held by them was entered. In other words, no act could be interpreted as connoting the establishment of relations with the invaders. The IAPC was to investigate "international," not "internal," affairs; though there might be some difficulty in determining whether Costa Rican rebels on Costa Rican soil were "foreigners" or merely "domestic revolters." (The same problem, under contrasting political circumstances, had arisen in Guatemala.) The viewpoint of the IAPC was summed up neatly by its chairman: "This, I hope, is going to be a lesson to the adventurers who have been lending themselves to any and every trouble in the Americas." The IAPC finally requested the rebels to withdraw, and on January 20 a demilitarized buffer zone was created between Costa Rica and Nicaragua. The invading forces shortly complied with IAPC's desire, and on January 22, after about twelve tense days, the little war was over.

The aftermath of the conflict did not find Somoza and Figueres any more kindly disposed toward one another. When Vice-President Richard Nixon visited Nicaragua about a month and a half after the termination of hostilities, Somoza embarrassed him by revealing

75

a deposit of arms allegedly used in the assassination attempt.* Somoza also charged the OAS with prejudicial treatment on two counts: first, it had blamed him inferentially though not specifically; second, it gave Figueres four planes at a time when he, Somoza, had none. Since Somoza had received on order from Sweden a shipment of twenty-five F-51 planes, his second complaint was hypocritical, to say the least. A State Department spokesman declared that there was nothing in these dealings to give the United States concern, but even though Somoza later explained that he planned to sell all but five or ten, it still gave Nicaragua the largest air force in Central America. Later, when talking with Figueres, Nixon discovered that he was as unwilling to compromise as was Somoza.

But after some deliberation, apparently both presidents decided that a more conciliatory spirit would be to their long-range advantage. They agreed to the establishment of a five-man commission to settle new issues that might arise between the two countries. The head of the commission is an American, in accordance with their request.

In the imbroglio of these two small Central American countries what significance is there for the security of the hemisphere? The Somoza maneuver combined elements of rebellion and invasion; however, no participation by a foreign power was involved officially. The Rio treaty does not provide for this kind of attack from *within* the hemisphere. Were international Communism involved, that part of Article VI in the treaty might be invoked which reads: "If the integrity or sovereignty or political independence of an American State should be affected by other than armed aggression. . . . " But, Communism did not figure in the Nicaragua-Costa Rican dispute, despite the invaders' efforts to label some of the members of the Figueres regime as "Communists."

The chief point to underline in the Nicaragua-Costa Rican affair is the importance it gave to a regional means for settlement of

*In October, 1956, Somoza was assassinated by one of his own countrymen. Neither Figueres nor any other Costa Rican was in any way implicated.

intra-hemispheric disputes. Since Guatemala had tried to confine its case to the United Nations, the OAS did not have the opportunity to conduct an investigation until the revolt ended all need for it. In the Costa Rican case, however, the OAS acted swiftly and effectively. In so doing, it not only heightened its prestige but also severely cautioned other adventurers—particularly military "strong men" disturbed over the proximity of a strong democratic regime—not to aid any would-be invaders. There were some who felt that the Rio treaty should be amended specifically to cover this kind of case. Generally it is agreed, however, that it would be unwise to tamper with a treaty so widely accepted at a time of enthusiasm for collective action. It would certainly be difficult to agree upon proper wording, and particularly in the light of the uneasiness caused by the Guatemalan episode, discussion might raise the old bugaboo of intervention. Furthermore, such change in the treaty might aggravate the cleavage between the authoritarian and the more democratic regimes. The will of the OAS to act collectively has proved more decisive than any juridical terminology.

The OAS might have more difficulty, however, in deciding on the proper course of action if there should be a revolt across the borders by democratic nationals against a repressive but non-Communist dictatorship in their country. To be consistent, it would have to enforce the rule as it did when a democratic regime was attacked. Yet such a revolt might be the only way for enlightened groups to rid their country of an odious dictatorship unrepresentative of the people. It would be interesting to see what the OAS would do in this not unlikely circumstance; the decision would not be an easy one.

There are, of course, other problems of hemispheric security, such as the perennial boundary disputes, especially between Ecuador and Peru, and the issue of sovereignty over territorial waters. Interesting from the point of view of international law, as well as important to the parties concerned, these problems are always in need of settlement, and at some future point may assume crucial significance. But at the moment, they are less pertinent to the hemispheric community as a whole than those we have discussed.

77

In summary, then, it seems that since 1947 the United States has felt that what primarily threatens Latin American security is not external nor even internal aggression, in the sense of one country or group of countries attacking another. The Rio treaty prescribes the proper measures for these instances, and the OAS seems able to carry them out. (Rather, the United States feels that Communist infiltration and subversion of government institutions) and public opinion are the real threat. The Communists in Guatemala, as they became more confident of their power, became more overt in their actions. A future pattern may be much more difficult to detect and will require constant vigilance both by the United States and the Latin American nations. This vigilance should also include drastic actions against subversive Communist activities, travel controls over known agents, and exchange of information among the countries, in order to root out the evil before it can flourish openly. Obviously such measures must be in addition to, not in place of, progressive alleviation of the economic and social conditions that nurture Communism. At the same time, general prevention must be undertaken by the inter-American community as a whole, in order to be really effective.

Unmolested, non-Communist revolts assisted by neighboring countries do not pose so critical a threat to security as Communist activities, but they do contribute to unrest, make the evolution of democratic government more difficult, and cause various nations (especially the smaller ones) to become disillusioned with the United States and the inter-American community. All this would help to fulfill one of the major objectives of international Communism, and for that reason, if no other, such revolts need to be handled multilaterally through an organization like the OAS.

Thus far we have discussed primarily political and diplomatic phases, many of which have had their economic and ideological aspects. Let us turn now specifically to economic relations.

-VI-

Trade, Loans, and Point Four

E conomic aspects have always been stressed in discussions of United States-Latin American relations; indeed many people feel that they are the most· important feature. Certainly rapid economic progress—a prime objective for Latin America—is closely related to social reform and achievement of a broadly based political structure. On the other hand, failure in steady economic progress is an important determinant in the trends toward nationalism, dictatorship, Communism, and anti-Yankeeism in Latin America. The United States inevitably must help its next-door neighbors achieve this progress. In this chapter, we shall consider the main economic problems and relationships and underline their pertinence to foreign-policy objectives. Because private American direct investment has an unusually great potential in furthering United States foreign policy in Latin America, and because unique factors involving human relations are involved in the direct investment of private American capital, this subject will be treated separately in the next chapter.

Apart from strategic raw materials and private direct investment, mentioned in Chapter II, the economic importance of Latin America to the United States is threefold: in trade relationships; in indirect, or portfolio, private investments; and in economic relationships with Western Europe and Japan, which contribute to Free-World prosperity. In recent years, American trade with Latin America has totaled about $6.5 billion annually, with imports from the area amounting to about $3.5 billion and exports averaging about $3 billion. The $.5 billion difference has been expended for interest on loans, profit remittances by American concerns, shipping and insurance services, and the purchases of certain goods made in Europe for which dollar payments have been

79

required.* Latin America would clearly buy much more of many kinds of goods from us if it only had more dollars.

In 1955, American indirect private investments in Latin America amounted to about $1.2 billion, chiefly holdings of national and state government bonds by American banks and investment houses and nonequity interests in certain private ventures. The role of Latin America in relation to Europe and Japan is chiefly as a provider of raw and semifinished materials (including minerals) in return for industrial products. Opportunities also exist for direct European and Japanese investments. It is obvious that Latin America economically depends heavily on the United States, which is its main market for exports, chief provider of imports, and principal source of public loans and technical assistance.

Although some consciousness of the importance to the United States of an expanding Latin American economy had existed before World War II, it was not until then that our government officials first became intensely preoccupied with the need to aid Latin America in rapid economic development. In part, this interest was motivated by a desire to increase the wartime supplies of strategic raw materials. There was also incipient consciousness of the fact that general development, particularly of manufacturing industries, would give rise to the creation of a middle class, which it was hoped would further political stability and the growth of democracy. During the postwar years of relative neglect of Latin America, less attention was given these considerations. Roughly since 1954, however, economic interest has been rekindled, in large part because of the recent political and social unrest in Latin America, dramatized by the Guatemalan episode and the suicide of President Vargas, and made mandatory by the threat of Communism.

---

*U.S. exports in 1955 to selected Latin American countries reveal some surprising comparisons with exports to European countries. The United States sold more to Colombia than to France or Italy; to Mexico and the Central American countries than to Great Britain *and* Scandinavia; to Venezuela than to Austria, Denmark, Ireland, Greece, Norway, Portugal, Turkey, Spain, New Zealand, Egypt, and Ethiopia *combined.*

The economic philosophy of the Eisenhower administration from 1953 through 1956 caused it to place primary emphasis on urging the Latin Americans to create an environment more favorable for private foreign investment. Also, after an initial disinclination to do so, the administration expanded the lending operations of the Export-Import Bank to provide capital investment which private sources cannot or will not provide for basic substructural services, or—as it is sometimes called—"social overhead." The reasoning apparently was that to attempt to remedy the manifold economic inequities would be a fruitless task, in any case a palliative instead of a cure. Instead, the concentration of aid on a few key spots in the economy, coupled with "sounder" financial policies and greatly increased private initiative, should within a reasonably short time cause substantial benefits to trickle down to the masses. The view has much to recommend it, but some cautionary notes should be sounded. First, it may be well to examine briefly the basic economic problems of contemporary Latin America.

As Henry Holland, assistant secretary in charge of Latin American affairs, pointed out in Boston in the fall of 1954, the principal economic fact in Latin America is the unprecedented desire of the common man for a higher living standard. In order to satisfy this desire, substantial economic development must take place. Actually, from World War II through 1955, an annual rise of 5¼ per cent in Gross National Product (GNP) took place in Latin America, but the average annual per capita increase in income was under 3 per cent. This is explained by the tremendous growth in population, between 2½ and 3 per cent per annum, which is twice that of any other major world area. The annual rate of all kinds of investment in Latin America, from 1946 to 1950, was about $6 billion, but in the latter year it began to decline owing, among other things, to a sharp fall-off in new American private direct investments. It is estimated that an annual productive investment rate of $7.25 billion is needed to achieve an increase of 2 per cent in per capita income.

In many Latin American countries, increasingly large groups are dissatisfied with the fact that their economies continue to depend primarily on the export of one or two raw materials, the prices of which often fluctuate considerably and for which the demand is inelastic. The proceeds garnered from these exports basically determine the external purchasing power to buy the many industrial and agricultural products which the countries do not yet produce. Latin American nationalists, abetted by Communists, maintain that, though political independence was achieved in the early nineteenth century, economic independence has not yet been attained. The extent of dependence on raw-material exports can quickly be seen: of the twenty Latin American countries, eleven depend on one commodity for over 55 per cent of their exports (five for over 75 per cent); for six others, two commodities make up over 50 per cent; in the instance of Peru, two commodities constitute slightly less than 50 per cent; and the bulk of Mexican and Argentine exports consists of 4 or 5 per cent.

Industrialization, which to Latin Americans means manufacturing, appears to be the only way for them to extricate themselves from this allegedly unfortunate situation. This, they feel, will provide their countries with insurance against the risk of being cut off from foreign industrial products in times of emergency, and at the same time will eliminate the high degree of dependence on fluctuating export prices. Such thinking, prevalent in much of Latin America for the last several years and bidding fair to continue, largely neglects agriculture. Because rural areas have generally received little attention from the national governments, which for the most part have devoted only small portions of their budgets to agriculture, production has declined. The large landowners often have not been interested in modernizing, and the small owners have been marginal and without influence. Cultivation methods and storage facilities are still largely antiquated, and adequate credit is lacking. These factors, added to the poor means of transportation, have caused the price of foodstuffs in the rapidly growing urban areas to increase sharply, thus contributing materially to the rising cost of living. Several of the countries have even been forced to expend precious foreign exchange on imports of foodstuffs, at least some of which they could feasibly produce. Outside experts have advised Latin American government planners to pay increased attention to production of more and better-quality foodstuffs and raw materials, including minerals, both in order to form a better base for their urban industrial areas and to increase their foreign-exchange revenues. In general, however, this advice has not been heeded. A few countries have initiated agrarian reform; but, except for Mexico, they have concentrated on the breakup of large estates without taking the other measures necessary to implement it.

Latin American nations seem intent on shifting from agricultural into industrial economies. Indeed, economic "transformation" seems a more precise way to express their objectives than economic "development." In the process, growth statistics are sometimes not too meaningful, since the entire economy is assuming a new orientation, one which may differ considerably from that of the older, more industrialized countries. For instance, the general absence of coal for development of an economically sound steel industry will be one strongly inhibiting factor. On the other hand, the probably continuing availability of large-scale intergovernmental loans, the possibility of air transportation, and the potential wide use of atomic power—all absent from the earlier industrializing economies—will certainly provide a different orientation.

In attempting this transformation, the governments are undergoing transition periods during which middle- and lower-income groups are more conscious of their basic economic insecurity than ever. The middle-income brackets are temporarily worse off than before, with severe inflations. The lower-income groups have made some progress but are now increasingly aware of, and acutely dissatisfied with, the wide gaps in income and status that still exist. To further the process of industrialization, the governments have invested heavily in industrial development programs. They have obtained the local funds for this development from deficit financing, from manipulation of central banking mechanisms, and from expansion of easy commercial credit; all these actions are in effect artificial savings. The proliferation of bureaucracies, the unnecessarily high proportions of many national budgets spent for military purposes, and the traditional tendency of Latin Americans to invest in real estate and other forms of conspicuous consumption have absorbed large funds that could have been used for more productive investment. Many Americans recommend a steeply graded, progressive income tax for Latin America, which it does not now have, but this might merely strip away much of the surplus private capital now concentrated largely in the hands of the wealthy few, without adding to productive investment. More useful would be greater efficiency in the collection of existing taxes and a system of tax credits to provide incentives for investments in certain industries.

Meanwhile organized labor, with increasing political power, has pushed hard for immediate economic and social gains, particularly various kinds of fringe benefits. On grounds of efficiency alone, recent surveys have indicated that the social problems of industrial progress, such as adequate housing, must be handled along with the purely technical and financial aspects. This has added measurably to the cost of industrialization.

To finance their "transformation" programs, the Latin American governments need relatively large amounts of dollars with which to purchase the needed capital goods and other industrial products. Since their exports do not provide them with sufficient dollar exchange, they must depend on loans and grants, supplemented if possible by long-term credits on imports, to fill the gaps. Many of the countries which request developmental loans most urgently suffer from the exodus of domestic capital into foreign currencies, especially dollars, that refuses to return home because of the unstable political and economic conditions. In 1956, there were roughly $3 billion of Latin American dollar holdings in the United States.

The most important source of dollars is obviously the United States' annual deposit in Latin America of $3.5 billion for purchased goods. Indeed, the maintenance of a high level of economic activity, with stable prices, is the single most important contribution that the United States can make to Latin American economic welfare. Oversupply and price fluctuations of their commodities are the principal headaches faced by Latin American exporters. The recent sharp rise and decline in coffee prices and the difficulty in disposing of cotton exports are the most recent examples, but sugar, copper, tin, lead, zinc, and wool prices also come to mind. Latin Americans complain that the United States urges them to expand production of many of these products in times of emergency. Then, when it no longer needs them in great quantity, and prices decline, the northern republic talks in terms of "free market" adjustment of prices. The perennial threat to imports of Venezuelan oil and Mexican and Peruvian lead and zinc naturally keeps these countries on edge. Also the largely uninformed hue and cry in the United States over alleged coffee "exploitation" by Brazil failed, as Brazilians point out, to take into account the periods when prices are discouragingly low.

Latin Americans fear that the United States is aiding the metropolitan powers of Europe to develop colonial Africa as a competitive, cheap-labor source of foodstuffs and raw materials. They also complain that the general trend in terms of trade (the trend over the years in the relative international prices of raw materials and industrial products) is against them. Actually, from World War II through 1956, the terms of trade substantially improved for Latin America, though the long-term outlook is dubious. It is estimated that about $11 billion have been placed at the disposal of Latin America through this improvement, but significantly, there has been no over-all increase in the volume of Latin American exports since 1948. The real difficulty is that, even with its growing population, the United States simply cannot use more than a certain quantity of most of the exports.

The other side of the coin in inter-American trade is Latin imports of greatly needed American industrial products. Because of the prevailing scarcity of dollar exchange, such imports have recently become a problem. The chief trouble is that American manufacturers, not so highly dependent on foreign markets as their counterparts in other countries, have been unwilling to grant commercial credits for longer than three to six months. This has proved reasonably satisfactory in several countries for light consumer goods, where the turnover is rapid, but not for the bulk of imports-capital goods and heavy equipment of all types.

Latin Americans, despite the large amounts of foreign exchange obtained by American purchases of their exports, do not tend to regard this as "aid," but rather as a normal commercial relationship. They look to bank loans and Point Four technical assistance for the supplying of actual aid.

LOANS AND GRANTS

From World War II through 1954, the United States sent to Latin America only about $1.1 billion in intergovernmental aid, as compared with about $47 billion (mostly grants) to the rest of the world. Most Latin Americans have been wont to cite this fact as proof that they have been badly neglected. Their attitude fails to consider the strategic imperative of granting huge emergency loans for postwar European reconstruction and later for combat against the growing Communist menace in Asia. In fairness to Latin Americans, most of them now see the picture clearly. They do, however, argue with some cogency that the aid to Latin America could have been a little larger, especially in terms of expanded and more rapidly processed intergovernmental loans.

Between them, the World Bank and the Export-Import Bank provided through 1955 the bulk of the aid, or about $1 billion, of which Latin America had repaid about $310 million. Contrary to ill-founded general impressions, the Latin American credit record has been excellent during this period. In the decade 1945-1955, twelve Latin American countries borrowed $642,405,000 from the World Bank, without a single default on payment of principal or interest. The loan repayment record to the Export-Import Bank has been equally good.

The Export-Import Bank, a United States government bank, makes loans tied in with American national interest. The World Bank, an international body, takes into consideration worldwide aspirations for economic development; however, the United States subscribes about one-third of its capital—and the incumbents in the presidency thus far have been Americans—which means that American influence is strong. The Latin Americans have strongly criticized the inadequacy of loans for economic development from both banks and the excessive delay in those from the World Bank. In particular, considerable pressure has been put upon the administration in Washington to expand the lending activities of the Export-Import Bank, and this expansion has now taken place. A number of factors have inhibited increased lending to Latin America, however, and will probably continue to do so. The principal ones are the poor credit standing of many Latin American governments because of inflationary burdens, faulty servicing of previous loans, the scarcity of technically and economically feasible loan projects, and the lack of local financing.

A method of overcoming at least one of these obstacles is through formation of a group such as the Joint Brazil-United States Economic Development Commission. The purposes of such a group, organized on a binational basis, are to formulate a well-devised plan of economic development, with priorities, and to screen loan projects carefully. This device makes available on-the-spot opinions of qualified American economists, engineers, and other technical specialists who spend enough time in the country to acquire a reasonably good understanding of its governmental structure, economy, and mores. Commissions like this may be intergovernmental, or the Latin American governments may hire a group of private experts on a contract basis. Such a procedure is not always feasible, however. The expense involved may be too high for the amount of the requested loans; sometimes there are complicating political factors. More loans will probably be made in the near future, but no torrent should be expected. Finally, one should always remember that strategic and political considerations sometimes figure as paramount in the making of loans, as has been suggested in Chapter IV and will be illustrated in more detail in the country case studies in later chapters.

POINT FOUR

Much has been written about global aspects of Point Four, the "bold new program." Appraisals have varied all the way from

glowingly optimistic estimates of Point Four's "revolutionary" capabilities to extremely derogatory statements concerning the "give-
away" program and its alleged lack of significant accomplishments.
Our own view is that while it has accomplished somewhat less
than its originators had hoped, still it has made significant headway in the relatively short time since its inception. Certainly the
Point Four program has become a vital component of American
foreign policy generally. Here we should like merely to explain
briefly what the characteristics of the program have been in the
last decade; to consider the significance of the program in Latin
America for United States foreign-policy objectives; and finally, to
discuss some of its specific problems and propose some solutions.*

Point Four is strikingly concrete. Unlike an information program, its progress can to a great extent be measured specifically.
In addition it can have long-range beneficial results that are intangible. People working shoulder to shoulder cannot help acquiring
a greater mutual respect and understanding, even though there
may be numerous irritations. Hence, Point Four can help to bring
about not only specific economic and technological achievements,
but also increased inter-American collaboration in other matters.
Latin America, far removed from the "crisis" areas of the world,
is thus not closely concerned in the military defense considerations
of the United States. A successful Point Four program, especially
in remote areas like Bolivia and Paraguay, may help convince
suspicious nations that Americans are not concerned solely with
military defense or with business. For example, how large a market
for United States products will Bolivia, Paraguay, or Ecuador
provide in the next decade? It must be kept in mind that Point
Four is an investment in human beings, a unique opportunity for
mutual broadening of insights. And it is by far the least expensive
component of the entire foreign-aid outlay of the United States.

The Soviet Union has learned well the lesson of Point Four;
indeed, has begun to apply something like it with at least some
success in underdeveloped regions. The recent Soviet offer of

---

*For most of these observations, the author has drawn upon his experience
in 1951-1952 as a Point Four program officer in Brazil.

$100 million of technical assistance to Haiti, including trained personnel to supervise the projects, is a warning that the Soviet Union may be planning to extend its own "Point Four" operations to the Western Hemisphere. Haiti turned down the offer, but it was a tempting one.

How much money and personnel have actually been invested in Point Four activities in Latin America, and what has the program consisted of in broad terms? Apart from emergency grants in recent years to Bolivia and Guatemala, and other grants earmarked for elimination of hoof-and-mouth disease and completion of the Pan-American Highway, about $130 million have been expended on the program in Latin America, from World War II through 1956. These funds, channeled through the Institute of Inter-American Affairs, were used initially for health and sanitation, agriculture, and vocational education, but lately have been applied also to public administration and several other fields. In the 1956 fiscal year the assistance amounted to $29,376,000. Nearly 900 United Nations technicians and contract personnel were working on assignments in Latin America, and about 1,800 Latin Americans participated in the training programs. Latin Americans have learned such varied skills as how to drive tractors, operate dragline earth movers, and use chemical testing equipment. Matching funds by local governments have grown rapidly in recent years—a point often overlooked by critics of the program. The Latin American nations in the 1956 fiscal year put up $50 million in their funds. If the goods and services provided locally are added, the contributions of the Latin American nations in 1956 were about two and a half times those of the United States. However, these contributions are always difficult to estimate, and country program directors are under pressure to make them appear as large as possible within reason, to impress economy-minded congressmen.

The program is based on bilateral agreements known as "basic country agreements," covering a period of three or five years. Usually the chief of the American field party sent to the cooperating country has been director of the *servicio* (the binational mission) and has reported directly to the minister in charge of the particular field of operations. The real Latin American counterpart to the American Chief of Mission has been the minister himself, insofar as the *servicio* is concerned, which generally has headquarters within the ministry. The minister, however, has naturally designated someone to be the "working" counterpart of the American chief, and complications have sometimes arisen as a result of this arrangement. By and large, however, the *servicio* system has been eminently successful, for example, in the Costa Rican, Paraguayan, and Peruvian agricultural, and Brazilian health, programs.

The technical cooperation program has its pitfalls, of course. First, by its very limited nature the program is long-range and unspectacular. Only in the noncontroversial field of health have rapid results been achieved. In the other fields vested interests combat in varying degrees the introduction of new methods. No dams or railway systems will be built as a direct result of this program; they will rather ensue from bank loans. Latin Americans chafe impatiently and some American technicians have been disillusioned with the slow progress. There are other problems. As health facilities grow and the heretofore crippling rate of infant mortality drops, the population increases by leaps and bounds. This requires not only an increase in the food supply, but also expansion of job opportunities in the urban areas. For both agricultural and industrial improvement, better management is needed, including marketing and accounting methods. Thus, Point Four enters the fields of public administration, business management, and productivity. Where does it stop?

In Brazil, the joint commission, itself in effect a technical assistance mission, discovered that, though new equipment was certainly needed, the problem of the key railway and ports aspects of transportation had arisen largely from poor organization. Therefore a training program for high- and medium-level railway administrators, involving tours of American installations, was initiated. In this way the modest Point Four program was tied in to the huge loan program. One expert went even so far as to say that, in a broad perspective, the basic problem in all aspects of Brazil's economy (except possibly power) was administration. Today one

90

of the two or three largest technical assistance programs in Brazil is in the field of public administration. A productivity center was also established along the lines of those in Europe, but it failed in its objectives and was discontinued. The basic problem appeared to be a lack of interest at this stage, on the part of influential Brazilians, in the objectives of the center, which were to show how to produce more efficiently at lower cost.

What should future American policy be toward the Point Four program in Latin America? It is pointless to make invidious quantitative comparisons with the funds allocated to other areas of the world. Southeast Asia and the Near East receive much larger sums principally because they are in more critically strategic locations. They may also, however, have different kinds of problems to tackle. Despite the seemingly low amount of money budgeted for nineteen republics (Argentina refused to accept Point Four aid), few people who have had experience in the program really believe that much more could be profitably absorbed. It must be remembered that the Latin American countries themselves must contribute relatively large sums, in terms of technicians and facilities, to the technical cooperation program.

Furthermore, the real problem is not so much money as qualified American personnel. Budgeted programs and projects are useless unless a sufficient number of American experts are on hand to adapt themselves to the country's customs and accomplish something of note in the short period of their assignment. The many months required by security clearances, with prospective employees finding more attractive alternatives in the meanwhile, are one of the major hurdles faced by Point Four administrators. Nor have the periodic changes of agency jurisdiction, the latest being the International Cooperation Administration (ICA), been conducive to a feeling of stability.

An interesting and much debated issue in technical assistance is the relative amount of emphasis given to the dispatch of American technicians abroad and the training of foreign nationals in the United States. Some argue that in the end the Latin American countries must do the job themselves. The best way to achieve the

91

desired "chain reaction" or "snowball" effect is for young men and women to spend at least a year in the United States in the field of their speciality. Older, more experienced "leaders" should also be sent for shorter visits. Upon their return these people will know better how to adapt to their native conditions than an American technician. This process may take longer, but will be far less expensive, and in the end will produce more solid results. Furthermore, it may have the added benefit of inculcating in these people a genuine pro-American spirit, something that has happened to the majority of such people who have trained for any real length of time in our country.

The other side argues that by far the greater emphasis should be on training people by demonstration methods and personal contacts on the spot. A prominent Latin American, the former Secretary General of the Organization of American States, Alberto Lleras Camargo, has suggested that the greatest single contribution to long-run Latin American progress which the United States can make is to provide more university-to-university relationships, whereby a few American specialists and a modest amount of equipment are sent to Latin American universities, particularly in technical and management fields. Here local young people, including some from modest income groups, avail themselves of the facilities. As things now stand, only wealthier Latin Americans can for the most part take advantage of training in the United States, which perpetuates the hold of the traditional elite on the economy. The arguments of both sides have merit; the answer, as usual, would appear to lie in a judicious combination, keeping in mind that each has its shortcomings.

The idea of university-to-university relationships appears to have caught hold in Washington in 1953, and a number of such have been established. This trend appears to offer great possibilities for the future; for example, bureaucratic red tape may be minimized by allowing the university a high degree of autonomy, and American universities themselves may gain substantially from this cross-fertilization. There are also problems, of course. Experience has shown that technical cooperation works well when an American university has a direct relationship with its southern counterpart, but not so well when it attempts to administer part of a going technical assistance program. The latter should be handled through a contractual group other than a university. Nor should the university take on any such assignment unless it is prepared to send well-qualified faculty members. This will not be so easy as it may sound, in view of the dearth of able professors, especially in the sciences and certain branches of technology, and the flood of students anticipated around 1960. To unload second-rate individuals on Latin American universities will merely cause ill feeling.

A few further admonitions seem pertinent. While technical assistance administered by the United Nations, Organization of American States, International Cooperation Administration, and private agencies are all greatly needed and should be welcome in Latin America, there should be constant vigilance to avoid unnecessary and wasteful duplication of effort. Although multilateral programs have their advantages in terms of international cooperation, we definitely believe that the United States should never terminate its bilateral assistance programs. This is not because, frankly, they operate more expeditiously with just two nationalities involved, but because the Point Four program is an integral part of American foreign policy toward Latin America. To administer aid entirely through multilateral agencies would be to dilute its effectiveness. In this connection, a carefully planned information program concerning Point Four activities in a given country addressed to nationals there is essential. Though care should be taken to avoid sensational publicity or bragging, it seems in our view equally unwise to efface one's actions completely. That is, if a majority of normally well-informed people in a given country do not know that United States technicians are contributing important services to health or agricultural or other activities in the country, something is wrong. In this era of constant self-criticism on the part of Americans concerning their foreign policies, their country should at least get credit where credit is due.

One particular type of economic operation extended to Latin America seems to hold considerable promise as a pattern for the future—either an outright gift of emergency foodstuffs or an exchange of foodstuffs for a raw-material export currently in excess supply, with payments in local currencies to be then utilized for economic development. Gifts were made to Bolivia and Peru, the former receiving $9 million and the latter $3.6 million. In Chile, the $5 million involved included among other considerations exchanges of wheat and copper. In this way the United States may partially dispose of its farm surpluses. Latin American countries may save precious dollars and use the local currency payment, partly to buy essential imports of other types, partly for development projects, and partly for the establishment of Fulbright study grants. Recently Ecuador stood as almost the only example of a Latin American country appearing to have as its principal objective not a rapid industrialization, but better development of basic facilities and of agriculture. In 1955 Ecuador requested a loan from the United States—so far (1956) not yet granted—of $2.3 million worth of wheat, cotton, and edible oils. It needs the funds for internal credits, with which it proposes to finance production of goods that do not compete with American products and to build roads. Serious consideration of such a sensible request would seem warranted.

One way in which South American countries could increase their dollar earnings substantially over present levels, as much as $200 million altogether by one estimate, is to expand their tourist business with the United States. The principal deterrents to tourist travel are the complex travel documents needed; the widely varying sanitary facilities; the scarcity of good hotels, especially in the interior; the lack of good highways and railway transportation; and the expense of air travel to South America, travel by ship taking too long for most vacations. Obviously some of these shortcomings reflect the retarded economic development and administrative problems facing these countries and cannot be remedied overnight. But air travel fares and flying times are constantly being reduced; it now takes only twenty-one hours to fly from New York to Buenos Aires, and by 1959 it reportedly will take only about seven hours. The South American countries can simplify the personal travel document requirements and make more effort, at least in certain urban centers, to establish uniform sanitary and health codes based on public health codes of the United States.

With these and other improvements, South America should be able to obtain substantially more than the approximately 3 per cent of total American tourist traffic expenditures that it received in 1954 and 1955. An illustration of the dazzling possibilities of tourist revenue is revealed by Mexico, where proximity to the United States and cultural renown admittedly are a great advantage. In 1954 and 1955, Mexico received around $250 million annually from American tourist expenditures, which is not far from the annual amount of dollars expended by Brazil on its petroleum imports.

An important contribution which the United States could make to develop Latin American initiative in economic development is to encourage regional thinking. Simón Bolívar's dream of a politically federated Latin America faded quickly and has never since been seriously revived, but in economic matters it might stand some chance of success in certain regions. The small Central American countries have long been divided by artificial economic barriers, including tariffs and differing currencies, and have suffered from parochial markets and limited resources. In recent years they have begun to take steps not only to create a modified customs union, but also to establish agricultural training schools and other facilities, each in a different country, to serve all of them. The Andean republics of South America might consider some moves along these lines. Possibly such an arrangement as an integrated steel mill industry might become economically feasible.

In September, 1956, Venezuela offered to contribute $33 million to the general economic development fund for Latin America, if the other countries would contribute corresponding percentages. This among other things might help further regional planning. Oil-rich Venezuela, however, stood alone in making this far-sighted proposal; many other countries, especially in South America, jealously possessive of their vital dollar reserves and strongly influenced by nationalistic drives, did not respond. Economic development will probably continue to be along national lines, and the United States will probably continue to provide most of the funds.

The United States, however, was distressed over the Latin American financial apathy toward the OAS. The northern republic contributed 70 per cent of the comparatively small budget, but many of the Latin American nations did not take enough interest to contribute their portions of the remaining 30 per cent. Through this organization, Latin Americans themselves could contribute some additional funds for mutual assistance. They might also, by the way of the OAS, devote much effort to the study of one another's problems and to common assistance, not only through money but also through technical advice.

Meanwhile, the fact that the United States has favored enlargement of Export-Import Bank operations and the establishment of the International Finance Corporation to expand both loans and guaranties of credit lines to Latin importers indicated that it realized other world powers were beginning to challenge its domination of the Latin American economic scene. The two groups primarily concerned were West Germany and the Soviet bloc countries.

Before World War II, Hitler's Germany was second only to the United States in Latin American imports. After the war, in 1947, West Germany had no exports to Latin America; but by 1954 its exports to that area had climbed back to great heights. Now it was Argentina's number one importer and became an important supplier to and investor in the Chilean Development Corporation. The Korean War frightened Latin America into buying manufactured goods from Germany on a barter basis. The Germans carried out an aggressive trade drive and practically in partnership with their government extended much longer term credits than American exporters, in some cases accepting payment in terms of investment concessions. Their exporters spoke Spanish and Portuguese well and adapted themselves quickly to the mores of the country. A Volkswagen factory was built in Brazil, and the small cars and buses made by this company were sold throughout Latin America. Yet Germany was still not satisfied. Whereas its record prewar year of $200 million in exports had represented 15 per cent of the total Latin American market, its exports in 1954 of $500 million represented only 10 per cent. The German competition was not necessarily adverse to American national interests, but it did point up the necessity for American exporters to improve their methods and adaptations to the major Latin American market. This did not mean copying German procedures literally. Luring buyers with easy terms of credit might in many cases tempt Latin American countries to purchase equipment that was not necessarily their first choice nor the best for their economies. Furthermore, such a close partnership between government and capital was contrary to the tradition of most American businessmen. Still some credit extension (perhaps up to a year) and improvement in "selling the Latin American market" seemed essential.

After years of almost negligible trade, the Soviet Union began in 1953 to make substantial increases in its trade with Latin America. In that year a total of $70 million worth of goods was exchanged, and in 1954 the figure was $200 million. By September, 1955, a total of nineteen Soviet trade deals, involving an exchange worth $500 million, had been made with Latin America. The most important trade agreement, with Argentina in 1953, included a two-way exchange of $150 million and credit of $30 million, on liberal terms, for purchase of Soviet capital goods. By 1956 several deliveries had been made both ways under this agreement, Argentina had agreements with many of the other bloc countries, and 13 per cent of its total exports were going behind the Iron Curtain. Most of the deliveries thus far, it is true, had been from Argentina to the Soviet Union; nevertheless, the 25 per cent fulfillment of the Soviet's quota of industrial equipment by 1955 was frankly more than many people had expected.

In 1954 Uruguay's greatest trade, for the first time in the history of any Latin American country, was with the Soviet Union. For its beef, mutton, hides, and wool exports, it received $11 million more than it would have obtained from prospective British buyers. In 1954 Brazil exported 1,000,000 bags of coffee and 100,000 tons of cocoa to Communist countries, in return for which it received, by 1955, 42 per cent of a promised delivery of cement, coal-mining and petroleum-drilling equipment, locomotives, and electric and Diesel motors. In 1954 Cuba sold 200,000 tons of its excess sugar to the Soviet Union at only slightly under the world price and also exchanged tobacco for light machinery from East Germany. In 1956 Soviet-bloc commercial representatives were touring the various islands in the Caribbean, receiving requests for needed goods and obtaining much valuable economic data. Czechoslovakian motorcycles had displaced British and German ones, and other bloc products were in evidence for the first time. In many cases Soviet machine tools proved to be inferior in quality; however, they might be perfectly suitable for certain Latin American factories and mills. In any case, they at least were better than nothing for countries in great need of equipment and without the dollars to buy them.

The over-all pattern appears to be that the Soviet bloc offers to buy raw materials at stable prices for a year at a time, supplying in return machinery on generous credit terms. (Thus far Communist China has had only a negligible trade with Latin America.) Is this increase in Latin American-Soviet-bloc trade necessarily sinister? Not immediately, but increasing Latin American dependence on the Soviet bloc for certain types of vitally needed equipment, such as oil-drilling equipment and tractors, may give the bloc an important toe hold in the Latin American economy, not so much in terms of quantity as in terms of strategic influence. Furthermore, these economic relationships might well mean eventually an increase in Soviet-bloc political and propagandistic capabilities. Some years ago, Eugene Varga, a Soviet economist, predicted the shift in Latin America toward economic coexistence with the Soviet Union based on a chart that he called "Agrarian Scissors of Latin America." This showed the line of the upward trend of inflated American industrial prices crossed by the descending line of agrarian prices in Latin America. As the blades of the "scissors" opened wider, so in the same proportion did the chances of Soviet economic relations with Latin America become better. Many Latin American countries engaged in increasing their trade with the Soviet Union might ponder this as yet unproved hypothesis, as might also certain United States officials.

What should be the general guidelines of our future economic policies toward Latin America, and how may these policies best serve our broad foreign-policy objectives? Merely to maintain present economic levels necessitates continued American purchase of Latin American exports. But it seems essential not just to maintain the present levels but also to raise them in order to enable Latin America to achieve that progress which increasing segments of its population earnestly desire. Furthermore, achievement of progress would make Latin America more stable and a greater contributor to the prosperity of the Western world. Imposition of tariff barriers and sharp price declines (especially of coffee) will have an adverse impact and should be avoided at all costs. Given the fact, however, that the United States does not have a state-controlled economic system, guarantees of industrial raw-material price ratios do not seem possible. To raise economic levels, the proposed expansion of development loans is necessary. There are, however, limits to the amounts of capital which most underdeveloped countries can absorb. Some expansion, and better coordination with the United Nations, in Point Four technical assistance is desirable, but care must be taken to grant this aid only when it appears that the receiving country really intends to make the most of it. Also, performance—and not constantly rewritten plans—is essential for the future; recurring disappointments may well have adverse effects on relations with the United States. Other concrete suggestions for improvement have been made earlier in this chapter. Most of the above affirmative recommendations were contained in Milton Eisenhower's report of November 18, 1953, to the President. The need seemed in 1956 not to be so much for new reports but for greater implementation of the suggestions in this one and in some of the many useful reports written by economic and technical experts of the OAS.

In view of the obvious fact that the United States will be able to satisfy only some of the economic requests of the Latin Americans, it should point out to them that it is not any lack of interest in their welfare which is responsible. It should explain that large "handouts" do not solve the real economic problems. Americans want to help the Latin Americans earn their own way, and this desire includes joint, though nonequity, partnership in the vitally needed development of their natural resources. Aid to Latin America will be to mutual inter-American economic advantage. In helping Latin America to industrialize, the United States builds up increased markets for its own industrial products. For some less complex goods there will be increased competition, but there will be an increasing demand for more intricate articles: fewer processed and semimanufactured items, but more capital goods. At the same time Latin America will gain. Whatever economic policies are adopted, the United States is bound to be criticized from some quarters, but at least this criticism should not be inspired by unenlightened policies. It should also be kept in mind that economic aid may sometimes have to be extended for obviously political reasons, for example, to help prop up a regime which, regardless of shortcomings, is attempting to do the best that can be done for its country in the face of great obstacles.

Some final thoughts seem in order. In 1955 the United Nations Economic Commission for Latin America (UNECLA) published a report on economic development in Latin America. The UNECLA report contained what has since generally been characterized as the "Prebisch thesis," named after the principal author of the report, Dr. Raúl Prebisch, a noted Argentine economist. Briefly, this thesis holds that the Latin American countries have been imprisoned by the inexorable workings of a process which condemns them to the roles of second- or third-class citizens in the modern world economy. It points out that the two-century-old industrial revolution has so far been concentrated in a few centers, especially the United States and Western Europe, with little effect on peripheral areas like Latin America. Indeed, there has allegedly been a long-run deterioration in the relative position of the peripheral areas.

Prebisch goes on to emphasize the need for vigorous action by the various Latin American governments to escape this inexorable process. For example, he suggests that in the future, approximately two-thirds of the outside capital needed for Latin American development come from intergovernmental loans and only one-third from private investments. This would be the reverse of what had happened from World War II until 1955. Obviously free trade and free enterprise receive short shrift in this thesis.

It should always be kept in mind that this report was written by a group of experts belonging to an international organization of great prestige. The report would clearly tend therefore to influence the thinking of Latin American political and economic leaders. It would not take a strong nationalist to juxtapose this thesis to Varga's "Agrarian Scissors" and emerge with an orientation hostile to the United States.

It is easy to find shortcomings in the Prebisch thesis. The industrial backwardness of Latin America is due in large part to the unfortunate legacy of three centuries of generally unenlightened Spanish and Portuguese colonialism (though one need not subscribe to the "Black Legend" in evaluating the period). This was the prime cause of the political and financial instability of most Latin American governments throughout the nineteenth and early twentieth centuries which obviously deterred economic development. Furthermore, the recurring disequilibrium in most of Latin America's balances of payments is caused by inadequate exports and flow of foreign capital into the area. This Prebisch noted, but he failed to point out that the chief reasons for these phenomena are the artificially overvalued currencies, which make Latin American exports more expensive, and the discriminatory regulations against foreign capital. Finally, it might be questioned whether the governments should do more, as Prebisch advises, or less. If they would simply provide for basic social services rather than enter into various businesses themselves, and provide better terms for foreign investors and more freedom of exchange, perhaps more might be accomplished. Obviously there had to be some compromise on all these matters, but at least the situation was not so black and white as the Prebisch report pictured it.

It is not sufficient merely to rebut the arguments of the Prebisch

101

thesis. Rather, Prebisch's concept should serve as a warning that all is not well in economic relations with Latin America. Some of these relationships are conditioned by the laws of nature and the economic facts of life, and are therefore not susceptible to change; but others are, and here attention should be concentrated, in order to make economic instruments the potent force for good which they should be in United States foreign policy toward Latin America. Among the most potent is the export to the southern republics of the dynamism of enlightened private enterprise.

-VII-

The Dynamism of Private Enterprise

Enlightened private American enterprise in Latin America can have a galvanizing effect not only on the economy but also eventually on the political and social structures of the southern republics. To most nationals in many Latin American countries the large American concerns are the real ambassadors of the United States. The dynamic flow of "know-how" and "show-how" is the most visible American contribution to the economic progress of these countries. An enlightened approach on the part of American business concerns works also to the advantage of the United States, by increasing admiration for American private initiative methods and giving the lie to anti-Yankee propaganda of local ultranationalists and Communists. In other words, by conducting itself in a way which will in the end redound to its own best self-interest, American business will at the same time advance the national interest of the United States. Because there already exists in Latin America both a large American investment stake and great potentialities for further investment, the southern continent serves admirably as a testing ground of private enterprise for the other underdeveloped regions of the world.

Of the total American overseas private *direct* investment of $17 billion in 1955, 40 per cent, or $6.2 billion, was located in Latin America. From World War II through 1955, new American investments in Latin America totaled $3.5 billion. These investments made major contributions to Latin American economic progress. Thirty per cent of all Latin American exports to the United States through 1955 resulted from American company operations, and American-financed factories contributed around 15 per cent of the total manufacturing output. A total of $1 billion was paid in taxes and $1.5 billion was saved by Latin American countries in

103

imports. There have also been many intangible benefits such as the dissemination of technical know-how, improved labor relations, and higher wages. Since 1948 the gross rate of return before taxes on private American investments in Latin America has been about 17 per cent. Actually in 1954, American investors earned considerably more in Latin America ($773 million) than they did in Canada ($584 million) where the investments, direct and porfolio, were 10 per cent higher.

The bulk of this investment has been in a certain few countries, especially Venezuela and Brazil, with over $1 billion in each. Moreover, all but a small proportion of the investment in Venezuela has been in petroleum, which accounts for by far the highest proportion of the investment stake in Latin America. Even in the case of petroleum, new American investment declined sharply in 1950, as did over-all direct investment, which figures on new American direct investments in selected years illustrate.

YEAR	MILLIONS OF DOLLARS
1947	442
1949	429 (358 petroleum)
1950	191
1951	187
1953	245 (663 to Canada in the same year)

Furthermore, in the period 1949-1953 only $15 million *net* new American private capital entered Latin America annually. A reinvestment of $300 million, some of it involuntary because of inability to remit, was made during this period. The small new figure reflects not only the slowing of the rate of new investment, but also the high dollar remittances, at artificially low official rates, of many American investments calculated on an expanded capital base. The profits in some cases have not been based on really higher contributions to productivity, but rather on over-valued, inflationary local currencies. The American companies merely took advantage of the remittances legally allowed them, but it is nonetheless true that the outflow of dollars has almost counterbalanced the inflow

104

in investments during recent years. (These figures do not reflect the real contributions of United States private investments in Latin America, as previously explained.) Thus, though it is true that Americans have their largest private *direct* investment stake abroad in Latin America, there has been only a relative trickle of net new investment southward in recent years. Something clearly / inhibits the flow. Before we examine the deterrents and possible incentives to further American investments, however, it is well to ask how private enterprise in Latin America can be of great importance in furthering American national interest in that area.

Most of the Latin American countries since colonial days have had a centralized, paternalistic approach to economic initiative. The governments, usually overstaffed and heavily concentrated in the capital cities, have had predominant roles in economic planning and development. The large national private enterprises have in the past been generally regarded with some suspicion as uninterested in the national welfare—which unfortunately most of them were. Before World War II, the bulk of foreign capital went into extractive and agricultural industries, especially mining, petroleum, sugar, and bananas, or into public utilities and transportation, particularly railroads. A number of these old-line foreign operations tended to be regarded as exploitative, and some were expropriated. Notwithstanding more modern policies adopted by most of these concerns in recent years, the legacy of resentment and suspicion remains. New concerns entering "with a clean slate" have an advantage in this respect. The improvement of many older enterprises and the infusion of new investment can do much to change the traditional ideology, which favors bureaucratized state control of the economy and manifests hostility toward private capital.

American enterprise can start a kind of "chain-reaction" release of private initiative, not only by setting an example of profitable but enlightened business practices for others to emulate, but also by stimulating the growth of corollary enterprises. Enlightened practices include more rational technological and administrative methods (a private Point Four program) and a greater sense of responsibility to the community as a whole, such as honesty in

105

paying legitimate taxes. Part of the "chain reaction" would be to introduce into the Latin American environment the notion of "risk" or "venture" capital (for which direct Spanish or Portuguese translations in the American sense of these terms do not exist). In general, Latin American businessmen have wanted to be practically assured of short-term high profits before investing—the old El Dorado which has come down from colonial days. To them "risk" capital is the kind one gambles with at roulette, and "venture" capital really means "adventure," of a highly speculative nature. The nearest Latin American terms are "capital to create capital" or "capital for expansion," but even these imply more of an element of chance than they do for Americans. The idea of reinvesting one's profits for the long-run gain in an enterprise which is not a "sure thing" has still to catch hold in Latin America.

An American company can have a major impact on a Latin American community by giving more job opportunities to lower-class, uneducated nationals. These should include vocational training and the possibility of promotion to responsible white-collar positions on the basis of performance, rather than on the more common Latin American basis of previous education, social status, and good connections. Good workers are needed more than top-level executives in Latin America; indeed, the scarcity of capable people to whom work may be *delegated* is perhaps the greatest single personnel problem in both governmental and business administration in Latin America. Furthermore, the education and promotion of lower-class people to higher level positions can indirectly bring about changes in the national school system and social mores and help to augment the usually small middle class. At the same time, American concerns should not bid competitively with the local governmental and business concerns for scarce professional talent and skilled personnel, nor should it pay salaries *much* higher than the going rate. This will merely incite unnecessary friction and jealousy.

American business must be careful, however, not to move too rapidly in introducing radical innovations. It must be sensitive to the social and cultural milieu. Interference in local politics must be avoided, though legislation affecting the status of foreign business in the country must definitely be of concern. American companies should seek no special favors not available to nationals, except of course the privilege to remit earnings abroad in dollars. After all, Americans are foreigners in a Latin American country, and their identification with the national patrimony is of necessity less than that of the natives. All they ask is that they not be discriminated against. The secret of good relations is to convince the government and people that it is not merely a matter of the company's contributing a good share of the profits to the government, but rather that the company and the country are in partnership to advance the national welfare. This principle has its pitfalls when the nation has a repressive dictatorship. Here the emphasis should be as far as is politically feasible on demonstrating that American business is concerned ultimately with the welfare of the people, rather than with that of any particular regime. In any case, American business should never intervene in the internal political affairs of the country.

The substantial reinvestment of profits within a country is another good practice for American business. Reinvesting will do much to convince our southern neighbors that Americans are not simply after quick profits to take home, but instead have confidence in the economic and political future of Latin America.

At this point an American businessman might well remind us that business by its very nature must always have as its primary objective the return of a fair profit to investors. Farsighted policies, however, will assure an even higher profit in the end. Conversely, unless business adopts such policies, the environment in which it must operate will not be conducive to its success. It is particularly important that the men sent down from the United States be carefully selected and trained, with the objectives of acquainting them with the over-all perspective and with the nature of the sensitive, nationalistic environment which they are entering. This most certainly requires some study of the history and culture of the country. In the end, of course, only actual experience in the country will determine who will really be adapted.

107

A few specific examples will serve to illustrate the impact of modern private enterprise on Latin America. W. R. Grace and Company is an export-import, industrial, and transportation organization, with a total capital investment of over $350 million. For a hundred years it has operated on the west coast of South America, with its widest range of business in Peru. It has made a fair profit over the long haul and its relations with the various Latin American governments have been good. In Peru, only one-half of 1 per cent of Grace's employees are United States citizens, or 50 out of 11,000. Many Peruvians occupy top-level positions, and there is little competition for jobs between them and Americans, because most of the latter are training for executive positions in the overall South American operations of the company. The workers have been given material advantages, including higher than average wages and fringe benefits, and an attempt has been made to inculcate in them a sense of responsibility toward company efforts. It has been discovered that labor protests increase as the standard of living rises, whether labor leaders are "left-wing agitators" or merely "business trade unionists." Therefore Grace has wisely used the services of social anthropologists, who report that the basic cause of the trouble seems to be the uprooting of the Indian and mestizo workers from their village communal structures and subsequent individual isolation in mechanized operations. In their new environment, two elements which were present before are lacking—a sense of self-esteem and a feeling of communion with the earth. Good management of employee relations has helped to remedy the first problem, and more emphasis on outdoor gardens rather than on the actual workers' houses has done much to instill in the workers a greater feeling of contentment. (The same type of restlessness and dissatisfaction among workers was discovered by a social anthropologist surveying the United Fruit Company's plantations in Guatemala.) The entire problem is much more than just worker welfare; it involves a society changing but still basically paternalistic, in which the legitimate interests of the workers are recognized without imposition of unreasonable restrictions on the operations of management. Grace has made it

108

a point to stay out of Peruvian politics and has cooperated with various government programs, though close contacts are maintained with appropriate ministries, and the company would certainly make representations to the government concerning any legislation affecting its interests.

After World War II, Sears, Roebuck and Company began expanding in the Latin American area. In 1955, it had twenty-six stores in five countries, on which it expended $26 million; in 1954, it grossed $79 million in profits. The total number of its employees in Latin America in 1955 was 6,000, of which only 100, or less than 2 per cent, were United States citizens. It has stimulated the growth of handicrafts and other local enterprises, and its sales of local products range from 35 per cent of its total sales in Cuba to nearly 100 per cent in Brazil. Sears has offered to the Latin American peoples a much wider choice of goods than they formerly had. New and more reliable products have been introduced, prices have been lowered, cash registers have been installed, and better advertising and night-and-day display techniques have been utilized. The use of coupon books on a consumer credit basis has proved successful, contrary to some pessimistic forecasts. The result of this revolutionary approach to the buyer in Mexico City, for example, has been astonishing to many, who had predicted that only the upper 5 or 10 per cent of the income brackets could afford to buy products at the Sears store. The actual percentage has turned out to be 50. Sears' broad effect is to aid in the growth of the Mexican urban middle class. At the same time the store has carefully followed the Mexican cultural pattern by letting the managerial staff help the employees paternalistically—for instance, through personal advice.

The Creole Petroleum Corporation has maintained excellent relations with the successive regimes in Venezuela. It divides its profits on a fifty-fifty basis with the government, in accordance with a 1948 agreement. Of the company's 14,000 employees, 90 per cent in 1955 were Venezuelan; and it has instituted programs involving training of nationals both in Venezuela and in the United States and their promotion to high-level technical and administrative positions. In 1954 Creole made a net profit of $239 million, or 24 per cent, having paid $104 million in wages and benefits to workers. It is easy to see why Creole has not had the trouble Anglo-Iranian had in Iran. The most interesting aspect of Creole's experience in Venezuela of late has been its community integration plan, whereby it has attempted to rid itself of some of its services (for example, housing and laundry) and to encourage promotion of local initiative along these lines. Not surprisingly, this "depaternalizing" process has not met with universal approval.

A final illustration is the employee-relations program of American and Foreign Power Company. Because a large number of accidents had been taking place, the company initiated safety and training programs, which became orientation courses concerning the employees' place in the electrical industry and that industry's place in the future of Latin America. The company realized that it ought to convince its own employees first, before launching a general public-relations program designed to attract the local financing that is so important to rapid expansion in this industry. The labor unions at first opposed the progress of the employee program, but they were later won over and are now among its strongest advocates. In Cuba, the Federation of Electrical Workers has expressed its confidence in the future of the company by investing $1.2 million of union funds in the bonds of the Cuban subsidiary. The federation also plans to rent to the company a large office building which it is constructing in downtown Havana. In Brazil, a fund-raising campaign, based on the desirability of local participation and the safety factor, netted $20 million. Thus a sense of local partnership is growing.

These examples, involving different kinds of operations, illustrate only a few of the ways in which American enterprise may influence the Latin American environment and in so doing may further American national interest. It is clearly desirable that new concerns enter the field and do likewise. Why, then, has private American enterprise not flowed toward Latin America in any substantial amount during the last few years?

American business alleges that the single biggest deterrent to

110

foreign investment in Latin America is the problem of converting local currency profits into dollars. In Brazil, for example, concerns during one period had to wait eighteen months before being able to convert. The inability to remit in many countries is due to their chronic dollar shortages, which in turn reflects the weakness of the currencies and the general political and economic instability. Convertibility guaranty insurance agreements offered by the Export-Import Bank and the Chase National Bank are a partial answer to this problem but do not strike at the root of the trouble.

Other deterrents are anti-Yankee feeling; legislation in some countries reserving certain fields exclusively or primarily for nationals (usually they are extractive industries, public utilities, insurance, transportation, and enterprises near national borders); legislation requiring the majority ownership and a high percentage of the employees to be nationals; government monopolies of certain activities (in Peru, for example, guano, tobacco, salt, alcohol, matches, playing cards, and explosives are government monopolies); "creeping" expropriation, involving unreasonable rate limitations on public utilities, restrictions on essential imports, unfair discrimination on taxes, and unreasonable labor laws; direct government competition; lack of basic services, such as transportation and power, and of an internal market; finally, double taxation (by the United States and by the Latin American country) of the company's foreign operations.

The former plight of the United States-owned copper companies in Chile, which produce half of Chile's incoming dollars, illustrates another type of deterrent. Since the copper companies had to pay the Chilean government 85 per cent of their operating income in taxes and exchange rate penalties, they were in effect subsidizing much of the nation's imported food. In 1953 President Carlos Ibañez put through legislation which left total taxes for the companies at 75 per cent of the production of that time, but like an income tax in reverse, progressively lowered taxes to 50 per cent of operating income when production was doubled. Soon afterward, the companies invested an initial $56 million in new and old mines and talked of doubling production.

111

The American and Foreign Power Company is one of long standing in Latin America, with real problems. Its investment there is about $1 billion. Though the situation has improved recently in some areas, the problems of this company still remain basically unsolved. For thirty years American and Foreign Power operated its electric power and tramway facilities in eleven Latin American countries; but it maintains that its net earnings have been less than they would have been in the United States, because of a combination of two factors: (1) the rates of return on invested capital have been low, because of government regulations. The normal gross profits on most other industries in many Latin American countries have been between 30 and 50 per cent, but power returns have been so much lower that the company has not been able to renovate its equipment consonant with complete safety requirements, much less expand; (2) the dollar values of its holdings have been reduced by declines in the dollar values of local currencies. This has reduced remittances to stockholders and made it more difficult to raise additional private capital in the United States. Instead, the company has to rely for half of its new capital on retained earnings, on a combination of Export-Import Bank and some private American bank loans, as well as on local government and private sources. Some of its methods of raising local funds were mentioned previously.

To what extent are all the above real deterrents to further private American investments? The government monopolies, outgrowths of a long-enduring tradition, are concentrated in only a few specialized fields. As for the nationalistic legislation—concrete evidence of the increasing trend toward nationalism—Yankee enterprises have decided that the wisest course is to keep harmoniously in step with the trend, through such measures as hiring more than the minimum number of nationals and promoting nationals to responsible positions. It is probably the better part of discretion, however, for future business not to invest in public utilities or railroads, or in large mining enterprises which furnish a high proportion of the country's foreign exchange. It is precisely in these sensitive fields that the nationalistic sentiment is most acute. Fields most promising for future investment are manufacturing and certain types of

112

agriculture, both of which would contribute substantially to Latin America's economic progress.

Anti-Yankee feeling, "creeping" expropriation, and discrimination have occurred in varying degrees in many of the Latin American countries and can be explained by two factors: nationalism, about which little can be done; and the past attitudes and policies of some American concerns, about which much can be done. Through better methods in handling government, public, and employee relations—methods such as we have cited—the antagonistic feelings of the nationalists toward American enterprises can be mitigated.

Actual large-scale expropriation on a legitimately nationalistic basis, without adequate compensation from the point of view of the owners, has taken place only in a very few instances; the two most notable are Mexican oil in the 1930's and Bolivian tin in the 1950's. The British had been operating the railroads in Argentina and some other countries at a loss and were not unhappy to be rid of them. Perón forced the sale of the American telephone company, but paid the price asked for it. Part of the United Fruit Company properties was expropriated by a Communist-oriented government in Guatemala but was returned after the revolt. There have been hints about nationalization of copper in Chile, but the government has followed the policy of obtaining as high a share of the profits of the companies without actually removing their incentive for remaining in the country. The Creole Petroleum Corporation seems safely established in Venezuela. All these enterprises fall into the category of public utilities or industries of vital national concern.

The one great stumbling block—convertibility—remains. In the final analysis, guaranty insurance agreements and Export-Import Bank loans to help meet dollar obligations are only palliatives. What is really needed is a greater flow of new private American capital to Latin America, coupled with intergovernmental development loans to remedy the lack of basic services and an internal market. This flow will help to alleviate the very conditions which now stem it. The trouble is, of course, that capital logically flows

113

in much greater amounts to those countries where there already is an abundance of dollar exchange for remittances. Success breeds success. Thus in recent years, Venezuela, Mexico, and Peru have been the chief recipients.

There will, of course, always be an element of risk in capital investment in Latin America, probably somewhat greater than in the United States. As Lleras Camargo of Colombia has pointed out, complete stability is out of the question in a continent which is changing and progressing. But the potential returns are high, and with the proper approach on the part of American capital, coupled with an intelligent nationalism on the part of Latin Americans themselves, investments can be attractive indeed.

The United States government can make them even more attractive by modifying the tax on foreign business operations. If it proves too difficult in the near future to change the tax legislation, the government should be more liberal in its interpretation of a legitimate "tax haven" or "profit sanctuary" in the several foreign countries requesting this kind of business. American concerns are allowed to remit their foreign dollar earnings to these "havens" without paying a United States income tax. The presumption is that they will then wish to reinvest these dollars in some other foreign country. Eventually they will have to pay a tax, of course, on any dollars brought into the United States, but it may be to their long-run advantage to postpone the remittance. The device may serve a constructive temporary measure, but in the long run new tax legislation seems imperative. Perhaps some lessons can be learned from a more thorough study of the Latin American partnership between German and Japanese private companies and their respective governments.

Many prospective investors from the United States have in the last few years been disinclined to investigate opportunities seriously, and ignorance regarding these opportunities has thus come to be a deterrent in itself. In March, 1955, an unprecedented gathering of American and Latin American businessmen took place in New Orleans to help dispel this ignorance. The meeting, called the Inter-American Investment Conference, was cosponsored by

114

Edgar R. Baker, managing director of Time-Life-International, and the late Rudolph S. Hecht, a New Orleans financier and one of the founders of the New Orleans International House. Months were spent on preparing the proper "climate" for this meeting. Over a thousand businessmen came to the conference, divided about evenly between Yankees and Latin Americans. This was the largest international meeting of leaders in private business to take place and also represented the largest number of Latin Americans who had ever come to the United States for a single purpose. All the Latin American nations and Canada were represented, and the amount of enthusiasm and preparation for the conference in some of the countries was surprising. Reports of the meetings appeared on the front pages of several Western European newspapers and over the Japanese national radio.

Several concrete achievements came from this meeting. A total of 375 investment projects, altogether worth $500 million, were presented. A known total of $125 million in new American investments was made, the largest being $56 million for a housing project in Venezuela and the smallest $65,000 for a limousine service to the airport at San José, Costa Rica. These sums take on an added importance when one compares them to the net new annual investment figure of only $15 million from 1949 to 1953. Other important projects included the manufacture of office equipment and the mining of manganese. Important for its long-range implications was the signing of contracts by the director of the International Division of the Southwest Research Institute at San Antonio for research in food, cattle, cement, minerals, chemicals, and petroleum.

In addition, an Inter-American Investment Trust was established in New York, with an initial capital of $10 million, which it was estimated would grow in five years to $100 million. This trust is of the closed-end type, with an emphasis on capital gains rather than income. It will buy direct equity investment securities from American companies operating in Latin America and from locally listed Latin American companies. A particular objective is to encourage medium and small investments. This is true also of the Investment Service Bureau in the New Orleans International House, which will act as a clearinghouse for information on investment opportunities. Finally, it was suggested that the laws of New York be modified to permit substantial investments in Latin America by insurance companies.

At the conference the Latin Americans became more thoroughly acquainted with the inhibitions to American investment in Latin America, and it was hoped that upon their return they would exert influence upon their governments to encourage the idea of private enterprise throughout their countries. The American businessmen not only learned of attractive business opportunities in the southern republics, but also met many Latin businessmen interested in private initiative. Evaluations of the results of the meeting have differed widely. Its sponsors and others felt that it was a success. It is only fair to point out, however, that many of the large concerns with Latin American interests have been skeptical about the usefulness of such conferences. Apparently they feel that enduring business relationships are not cemented in the fanfare of a big conference. Nevertheless, it would seem at least to have facilitated manifold initial contacts, some of which might eventually become fruitful.

Nobody acquainted with Latin America expects the climate for American private investments to transform itself magically overnight. Nationalism probably will continue to be strong; habits of paternalistic government will remain. Even apart from this, it is obvious that, despite all the good that it can do, American capital cannot solve the world's economic problems by itself. Intergovernmental development loans will continue to be necessary to furnish social overhead capital and establish basic services, without which private capital, either national or foreign, will not be able to operate satisfactorily. The over-all national strategic and political interests of the United States, and of the hemisphere, may sometimes have to dictate American governmental policies which will be the controlling influence. Yet, there is no reason why the interests of enlightened private American business should not complement governmental policies and reinforce the best American national interests. The two can work in collaboration with their Latin American counterparts in any given country.

A final thought may be in order, addressed primarily to those who have been critical of the past performances of some of the large American business corporations in Latin America. Undeniably the history of these operations reveals much to criticize, although they were considerably better than the practices of native Latin American businesses at the time. A great deal can be learned from mistakes of the past, but little is to be gained by raking over the coals. Most American concerns, with new public- and employee-relations programs, are entirely different from what they were two decades ago, and are constantly adapting themselves to the changing Latin American environment. The major contemporary American interest in Latin America emanates from business, and it has a direct impact on the lives of many thousands of Latin American citizens. Not only can it contribute to the forging of closer economic and political bonds; it can also play a part in bringing about a better mutual ideological understanding.

117

-VIII-

A Meeting of the Minds

Prior to World War I, international relations were generally divided into three categories: diplomatic, political, and economic. In modern times a fourth dimension has been added. Various terms have been used for it, including "cultural," "psychological," "emotional," even "moral" or "spiritual"; but "ideological" seems the most apt. The United States has only recently begun to explore this still nebulous realm and is therefore inexperienced in it. Some Americans question seriously the usefulness of this phase of our contemporary foreign policy, which they usually call "propaganda." Yet even they will admit the importance of at least making available to foreigners books and other materials that give a true picture of the United States. Very few are therefore opposed to the establishment of libraries and information centers abroad. At this point, however, critics divide. Some would stop simply at information; others would go on to carry out an elaborate program involving the use of various cultural media, seminars, and other devices. Disputes arise over the relative emphasis on anti-Communism and pro-America. We cannot attempt to explore here all the complexities of this moot subject, but we can try to determine precisely the objective of an information program.

Usually the objective is expressed by the cliché, "a battle for men's minds," between the Communist side and ours. We suggest that this is misleading; that the United States should not really try to "win men's minds," in the sense of pressing foreigners to accept American values. Rather, it should attempt to gain a *fair hearing* for its side; to enable people to make up their own minds on the basis of accurate information. The real objective may be called a "meeting of the minds." Implicit in this, of course, is the assumption that given a fair hearing, the United States' philosophy

118

will have the advantage. A clear understanding of the American way of life and foreign-policy objectives can lead to enduring respect and prodemocratic orientation, if not always close ties of friendship. This most emphatically does not mean that the United States should try to remake other countries in its own image. They, too, have had experience with the intricacies of human nature, and Americans have much to learn from them in this regard.

What this country is basically trying to convey to the leaders of opinion in foreign countries, then, is a sense of shared destiny, and the messages put across abroad that can help that sense. But at the same time great care should be taken, especially in the so-called underdeveloped areas, to assure the intellectual leaders that there is no intention of superseding their culture. Put another way, they should be confident that their cultural leadership is not imperiled by the leadership of the United States.

Despite many areas of friction, the United States has this desired sense of mutual understanding and respect with the countries of Western Europe, particularly with Great Britain, where the ties of common language and historical antecedents are strong. The same communion is not always to be found, however, with most of the other areas of the world. Since Latin America is an integral part of the West politically and economically, achievement of mutual understanding with its great northern neighbor should not be difficult. But an Asian type of fatalism and estheticism held by many in the Indianist countries of Latin America, and the differing temperaments, backgrounds, and outlooks in the other nations make this more difficult than it appears. It would probably be more feasible to study each country (or region) carefully and then adopt the program best suited to its characteristics, rather than to attempt one global approach. For example, Brazilians and Argentines certainly differ from one another in their receptivity to American influence; and even within a country, different problems may require entirely different kinds of treatment.

Any information program for Latin America will probably find that the most serious obstacle facing it is anti-Yankeeism, or Yankeephobia. In recent years increasing nationalism, stimulated

119

by Communist propaganda, has given rise to frequent resentment toward the United States, sometimes aggravated by ignorance or misinterpretation. Indeed, the underlying tensions occasionally flare into violent manifestations, for instance, in the anti-American demonstrations (mostly by students) in Uruguay, Chile, and Mexico, following the Guatemalan episode. These ostensibly were precipitated by the feeling that Yankee intervention had taken place. More disturbing for their long-range implications were the anti-American riots in Brazil incited by President Vargas' inflammatory suicide note which blamed Brazil's woes on foreign economic interests. Though Communist action increased the tensions, Yankeephobia clearly had existed for some time. This was particularly startling in a country that traditionally had been a great friend and ally of the United States. Three of these four countries, incidentally, are among the leading democracies of Latin America, and one, Mexico, has strong influence over the rest of Latin American opinion.

What are the historical roots of anti-Yankeeism? It is not new in Latin America; it goes back at least as far as the turn of the century. In a deeper sense, it is simply the modern manifestation of the xenophobia from the colonial period a century earlier, when the native-born *criollos* were resentful of the Spanish *peninsulares* who ruled them. Considerable admiration for the American political system did exist during the early years of Latin independence in the nineteenth century, but the Panama Canal and the Caribbean intervention, as we have seen, stirred up considerable resentment against the United States on the part of Latin American leaders of opinion. After World War I, this feeling continued, together with a sense of exploitation at the hands of American business interests. With the Good Neighbor Policy, much of the resentment again subsided.

Though the United States' nonintervention promise made in 1933 at Montevideo played an important part in creating good will, fully as important were the ensuing positive manifestations of Yankee good will and attention. Citizens of the United States began to make a real effort to understand the Latin American

120

culture and way of life. Notwithstanding the partially justified criticism regarding the "superficiality" of that era, this basic fact should be kept in mind.

What most thoughtful Latin Americans resented and feared from 1900 to 1933 was that the United States, growing more aggressive as it became more powerful, was yet culturally immature and therefore unable to comprehend the humanistic and esthetic values which existed in "backward" Latin America. Because of the mechanical efficiency, technological accomplishments, and organizational ability of the United States, its "Protestant, Anglo-Saxon, materialistic" way of life tended strongly to influence the Latin American people; and might eventually engulf the "Catholic, Latin, humanistic" civilization of Latin America. José Enrique Rodó of Uruguay in his famous allusions to Ariel and Calibán (Latin America and the United States), the Nicaraguan Rubén Darío in his fiery poems, Manuel Ugarte of Argentina in his *The Destiny of a Continent,* José Vasconcelos of Mexico, and other influential intellectuals inveighed along these lines against the "Colossus of the North."

With the advent of the Good Neighbor Policy and then World War II, the feeling of being misunderstood and treated in an entirely utilitarian way was submerged in the mutual flow of friendliness. Since the war, however, Latin Americans in general have once again come to feel resentful and cynical about the policies of the United States towards their region. Now it appears to many of them in retrospect that the era of good will was only an illusory interlude in an enduring continuum of basically distant relations between the two Americas. Both in terms of specific economic neglect and in terms of general American misunderstanding and disregard, Latin Americans feel much as they did before.

Meanwhile, the extremely rapid urbanization in many of the Latin American countries has brought to the forefront new groups which are now the primary molders of opinion in Latin America, and which at the same time are the chief propagators of the new nationalism. Their attitudes toward the United States are therefore

121

of crucial importance. Though much more needs to be known concerning the composition and the opinions of these groups, enough information has become available to make a general analysis possible.

Most of the new Latin American molders of opinion live in large cities. Generally their social background is different from that of Rodó and his generation, and reflects the changes that have taken place in the half-century since then. The earlier molder of opinion, an intellectual of some depth and integrity, led a leisurely existence suitable for scholarly and academic pursuits, often made possible by an income from landholdings or export revenue. Though he expressed himself intellectually to the contrary, he felt emotionally close to the landed gentry. Today the way of thinking of the new molder of opinion is conditioned by the values and norms of an industrializing and urbanizing society. He is likely to be a bureaucrat, journalist, urban labor leader, army officer, or possibly an industrialist—in other words, a member of the new urban middle group. He has little time for leisurely academic or scholarly pursuits, partly because he must often hold several different jobs. The university seems to participate in the active political arena less vigorously than before, yet it still contributes heavily to the intellectual and ideological formation of Latin American youth, who have traditionally been much more politically minded than their American counterparts.

Relatively few of the new opinion leaders, especially bureaucrats and labor leaders, visit the United States, because of either financial limitations, or mere lack of interest or incentive. Few labor leaders, except perhaps in nearby Cuba and Mexico, have close friendships or contacts with American labor leaders. Almost completely absent from Latin American universities are courses on the economic and political systems of the United States, its history, or its culture, with the result that intellectuals and labor leaders have little appreciation of the culture of the United States, as distinguished from its purely economic and technical accomplishments. In recent years, growing numbers of these people have been making trips behind the Iron Curtain.

To a considerable extent anti-Yankee sentiment in Latin America is part of the trend toward an insular nationalism, which in one sense compensates for an underlying feeling of insecurity and lack of real achievement. Apart from political and economic frictions and misunderstandings, however, channeling of nationalistic feeling against the United States is intensified by an increasing apathy toward American democratic ideals and by certain serious Latin American misconceptions or inadequate comprehensions of the United States. Additional aggravations may come in the form of injuries to personal feelings in Latin Americans' contacts with Yankees.

Perhaps the most serious contemporary ideological problem between the United States and Latin America is the apathy, prevalent in many influential Latin American circles, toward the American system as a dynamic and progressive example of the democratic spirit. Once the United States was the chief purveyor of enlightened ideas and innovations to Latin America. The following statement, made by the chief of the eighteenth-century revolt against the Spanish colonial authorities in what is now Colombia, seems strangely dated: "Let's send them to Philadelphia to learn the new philosophy." International Communism and Fascism in recent years have seemed to provide the chief revolutionary stimuli to Latin American innovators. An impressive analogy can be drawn between the persistent export to Latin America of the French revolutionary slogans of Liberty, Equality, and Fraternity, after Napoleon had taken over dictatorial control in the early nineteenth century, and the present-day vitality that the Kremlin's appeals for freedom and equality for the oppressed masses continue to hold for many Latin intellectuals.

This is not to say that most intelligent Latin Americans do not know that the United States is a democratic country, but the force of its example is not so great as it used to be. Part of the trouble obviously arises from the fact that our revolutionary origins now seem rather remote. For many years the United States has been evolving, generally in an economy largely free from central direction, toward a highly industrialized democracy. Latin America

123

and other underdeveloped areas find it hard to discern the essence of this evolutionary approach. The dynamic *élan vital* of the Communist movement is easier to perceive, though this does not mean that they wish to imitate this "ism" in their own countries. Yet the "American dream," including the allegedly naive morality and "do-gooding" spirit, has by no means faded and, if properly presented, still may greatly appeal to Latin American thinkers on idealistic grounds. In this respect, the United States has a great potential advantage over older European powers in its international relations, but skillful handling is certainly required.

The prejudice and discrimination in the United States against people of mixed blood are an "Achilles' heel" for Communist propaganda in Latin America as in most of the underdeveloped areas of the world. Though often not discussed openly with Americans, prejudice is frequently present in the minds of Latin Americans. Particularly as shifts in social structures and cultural levels bring more people of mixed blood into the ruling groups, sensitivity on the point may increase between Yankees and Latin Americans. Although this source of friction is unfortunately based on a reality in American life, two fundamental misconceptions aggravate it. One is an almost complete Latin American ignorance of the historical background of the Negro problem, in particular the tensions engendered by the Civil War and the Reconstruction Era. The other is an inadequate comprehension of the substantial progress that has been made toward solving this problem during and since World War II. Especially in view of a new Soviet propaganda emphasis on American prejudice and scorn toward mixed races in Latin America, greater Latin American understanding of this "American dilemma" and of the sincere efforts to solve it is essential.

Despite rapid social changes in some of the larger cities, Latin Americans generally still place great emphasis on maintaining the family or clan unit intact at all costs as the basic pillar of society, and on this score their impression of American social life is hardly favorable. They regard with aversion the often fragmented family life, the frequent divorces, the positions of seeming equality and sexual freedom accorded women, heavy drinking, and nervous tensions. Such characteristics of the highly industrialized, urbanized complex in the United States tend to make the Latin Americans wary of becoming more "Americanized."

Basic in Latin American attitudes toward Americans is an inferiority complex. Envy of greater American wealth and accomplishments, racial sensitivity, sometimes even poor personal health, all go to make up these feelings of inferiority—and unfortunately they are often abetted by a superiority manifested explicitly or implicitly by some Yankees in their contacts with Latin Americans. Few American government officials have any prior knowledge of or interest in the history, culture, and languages of Latin America, but most make a commendable effort to adapt themselves to the native customs and to learn something about their assigned country. The principal aggravation comes rather from the residents of the American colonies in Latin America. These Americans, having no feeling of permanence as do the Germans and (now) the British, look condescendingly upon the "natives," generally refrain from social contact or intermarriage with them, and often politely ostracize the Americans who do associate principally with local inhabitants. All too often the American colony is identified exclusively with the "country club set." It is only fair to add that behavior of this kind may be natural to a foreign colony from a more powerful and economically advanced country. One must also consider that in most Latin cities, Americans and other foreigners are not generally invited into homes of nationals, and must take the initiative themselves. Yet this problem is unquestionably one of the major irritants in Yankee-Latin American relations.

The problem of social barriers has a peculiar complexity in Latin America, as compared to Europe or Asia. Europeans, feeling culturally superior, often do not care whether the American colonies in their countries mix with them. Asians apparently have an inferiority complex but also maintain a kind of oriental "East versus West" solidarity, reinforced by highly developed religious philosophies. Latin Americans have no such props; their countries after all are simply somewhat neglected offshoots of Western civilization.

125

Our southern neighbors are generally their own greatest critics and do not need the shortcomings of their political and economic systems emphasized. In particular, they know that extensive corruption in their governmental systems is among their greatest problems. They may perhaps be pardoned for feeling a little better about this affliction when they read about the venality of some American political machines. They would at least greatly appreciate recognition by American critics that many Latin American leaders are not corrupt and are doing their utmost to introduce reforms. Moreover, Latins resent the extremely limited coverage they receive in the American press and periodicals, and complain with some justice that only revolutions or other sensational events seem to make the news in the United States.

Generally the economists and other government officials of the southern republics are inclined to be more theoretical and doctrinaire than their American counterparts. Often they are literary men with considerable imagination, given to broad concepts and plans, to what they call *proyectismo*. Their erudite but often emotional discussions range over a multitude of subjects. If these Latin Americans are dealing with American counterparts who are concrete, practical, and chary of broad generalizations, it may well be difficult to achieve a "meeting of the minds." These Latins complain that Yankees often do not understand broad integration and synthesis; and Yankees in turn feel the Latins frequently live in the realm of pure speculation. Furthermore, the Latin American often finds the American to be cold, impersonal, "organized," and impatient. To the Latin American, the way something is done is often as important as what is done, even if it entails considerable delay and a lot of paper work. Even though the northern and southern approaches appear to be gradually drawing closer to one another as Latin America industrializes, the gap remains.

Thus, we may ask what broad constructive approaches might bring about stronger bonds of friendship and understanding? First, it should be emphasized that much of the anti-American sentiment will continue, no matter what policies are pursued by the United States. Given the probably continuing frustrations of

126

Latin American nationalists, and the great disparity in power and wealth between the United States and Latin America, a certain amount of resentment and misunderstanding seems inevitable. The United States should not lament its unpopularity, however, but rather view it philosophically (though not complacently) as part of the price a powerful nation has to pay for its position of importance and leadership in world affairs. Great Britain was certainly not overly popular in many areas during the nineteenth century, but this did not appear to worry its citizens much as long as their country was respected. Americans must guard against making too strenuous an effort to "sell themselves" merely in order "to win friends and influence people," an effort which so often smacks of hypocrisy and can easily produce an effect contrary to that intended. Prestige and respect should be the coveted goals.

Nevertheless, the United States government can help to alleviate resentments and correct misconceptions, especially among those relatively few people who are the real molders of opinion in most of the countries. Through the United States Information Agency's fifty-one information centers in Latin America, with their 75,000 students of English (1955), and through other cultural media, mature explanations concerning American civilization can be presented to general audiences. Few Americans appreciate fully the importance of the American cultural centers in their local Latin American environment. Some of those establishments are as large as good-sized American universities; the largest, Casa Roosevelt in São Paulo, has about 7,000 enrolled in English lessons and courses concerning the United States. Equally important is the establishment of chairs in "American Studies" at perhaps half a dozen leading Latin American universities. Eminent American professors or writers should be given incentives by the State Department and the USIA to fill these chairs. Thereby an influential audience of intellectuals, who would not be likely to frequent the cultural or information centers, could be reached. Among the serious misconceptions the professors can dispel is that the American economy is largely dominated by a few monopolistic

127

concerns which have unenlightened labor practices, an impression gained in part from dated American polemical literature. These professors should have a good knowledge of the historical, political, economic, social, and cultural evolution of the United States.

At a more popular level, books explaining American history, economy, and government can be made available—at a low price so that thousands of readers who would not otherwise be able to purchase them may do so. It is heartening to note that in 1955, the USIA assisted a Buenos Aires publisher to produce 42,000 copies each of *The Great American Heritage* and *American Capitalism* in Spanish for distribution throughout Latin America. Also *The USA—Its Geography and Growth,* a USIA book, was adopted by the Cuban Minister of Education as a textbook for Cuba's high schools. (An American professor of Latin American Studies can only wish that a corresponding work on Latin America were made the basis of a required course on the area in American schools.) Books and pamphlets of this nature can not only increase the Latin Americans' knowledge of American institutions, history, and geography, but can also further understanding of the United States' very real cultural and esthetic contributions.

Americans must bear in mind the nature of the people to the south. Latin Americans are extremely proud of their great national and cultural figures, and gestures such as the unveiling of statues, dedication of monuments, and commemorative celebrations have a tremendous impact upon the emotional Latin temperament. Generally, visitors from the United States, even Americans in general, have tended to slight this aspect of the Latin character. Though commemorative sessions, usually connected with the Pan American Union, have been held in official Washington circles, and visiting dignitaries in various Latin American countries have on occasion helped in celebrations, more widespread attention in the United States could be paid to great Latin American historical figures and holidays. It would be particularly valuable if such attention could come from private groups in places other than Washington, such as that paid by Pan-American societies, especially those in New York and Boston.

Moscow—for her own motives, of course—has gone a step beyond the United States in making use of the Latin Americans' nationalistic feelings. In 1953 a celebration took place in Moscow to honor the hundredth anniversary of the birth of José Martí, the highly revered patriot hero of Cuba. Phrases such as "Fighter for freedom from oppression" were employed, letters of tribute were read from Jorge Amado, the Brazilian social novelist, and Pablo Neruda, the Chilean poet— both of them Communists, to be sure, but also highly esteemed throughout Latin America. Exactly how great an impact such obviously cynical gestures on the part of the Soviet Union may have on non-Communist Latin Americans is difficult to estimate. Nevertheless, the United States can certainly assume more initiative in these matters.

Both the United States government and private enterprise can enhance mutual understanding by screening more carefully the personnel they send to Latin America, with a particular eye toward adaptability to Latin American customs and willingness to learn the language and something of the history and culture of the country to which they are assigned. It would help if the State Department and the USIA, the key government departments in this intercultural process, were to encourage the idea that specialization in the Latin America area and its languages affords opportunity for a promising governmental career.

The many Yankee businessmen who travel to Latin America can help greatly to give Latin Americans a better impression of the United States. Naturally the main activity and purpose of the trader is to discuss sales data. The Latin American, however, is generally more given to discussing world affairs than is his northern counterpart. He often queries the Yankee about current developments in the United States and can hardly be blamed for occasionally needling him about "Yankee imperialism" in Latin America. Unfortunately he sometimes obtains an impression that his northern neighbor is shallow, self-centered, and interested only in conversational banalities. If the Yankee trader will learn something of the history of each country he visits, and will add to that some knowledge of the history of past American relations

129

with Latin America, he may surprise his southern neighbor, and at the same time can meet the Latin on equal grounds in his discussion of "Yankee imperialism." He does not need to apologize for Yankee actions nor be critical of his country or fellow-countrymen beyond a certain point. What he can be prepared to do is to explain. For example, much good can be accomplished by explaining that, contrary to Hollywood-inspired impressions, most Americans lead a civilized, wholesome life! The American businessman can also clarify his own status, pointing out that American entrepreneurs live in an ambitious and competitive community at home, which has as one of its chief characteristics the enjoyment of accomplishment. As for the American colonies in Latin America, fortunately more and more Americans are coming to see that they can at once be proud of their own country and appreciate values in the native society.

The program for cultural exchange of persons is and can in the future be of great value. In view of limited budgets the really influential opinion-formers should be invited to the United States, with time to look at the country leisurely and thoroughly. In particular, increasing numbers of influential labor leaders should be invited. One obstacle is the difficulty some non-Communist but leftist labor leaders and intellectuals encounter in fulfilling visa requirements. Naturally great care must be exercised to protect American security interests, but if some of these influential people (who are receiving invitations from the Soviet bloc, incidentally) were allowed to see the United States for themselves, they might return less "leftist" and more pro-United States. In addition to high-level people, the State Department and private organizations should also from time to time invite popular cultural, sports, and entertainment groups to come to this country, and should send corresponding American groups on tours of Latin America. Such intercultural contacts can have a powerful impact. A precaution to be taken in administering this vital program deserves special mention. Latin Americans of noticeably mixed blood should be sent to those parts of the United States where the possibility of personal affronts is minimized. This has unfortunately not always

130

been done. When unpleasant experiences occur with Latin Americans, as with Asians, the United States loses friends rather than makes them.

American newspapers and periodicals answer charges of scant news coverage for Latin America by saying that most of their readers have little or no background concerning the area and therefore no interest in it. Yet if the large dailies or weeklies were to publish a few "background" articles on Latin America, they might find that considerable reader interest has been stimulated. Moreover, establishment of Latin American institutes in American universities would be a great boon to this stimulation, because they would provide potential newspaper readers with that desired background on Latin America.

One item cannot be omitted in any consideration of ideological relations—Hollywood movies. The mass popularity of the movies in Latin America can hardly be overstressed. All kinds of films, good and bad, on every conceivable subject generally attract sizable audiences, not only in the large urban centers but also in the rural towns. The intellectuals, as in the United States, scorn the great majority of Hollywood productions, and tend to patronize European films almost exclusively. But the rest of the population enjoys them greatly, and so far as can be determined, do not really get a bad impression of the United States, though it is obviously distorted. Many Americans abroad, after seeing a number of stateside movies of poor quality have expressed the wish that movies sent abroad could be screened beforehand. With the American aversion to state controls, however, and the difficulty of establishing acceptable criteria of good and bad, this does not seem feasible. One effect which Hollywood movies undoubtedly have is to stir up ambition for more material possessions, for more freedom for women, and for many other things—ambition which may well be frustrated. In this sense, then, movies are an unintended ideological force.

No treatment of ideologies can be complete without some comment on the role of American missionary enterprises in Latin America. Through their missionaries, Americans reveal themselves to Latin Americans as people of genuine religious faith and also affirm the world-wide membership of their various denominations. Both Protestant and Catholic missionaries can collaborate in kindling the Christian spirit in Latin America, which is a powerful spiritual antidote to Communism. In view of the severe shortage of priests in most Latin American countries, this kind of American activity has generally been much appreciated, particularly, for example, in huge Brazil. Both sects, however, should remember that their representatives are still foreigners who must tread gently in this delicate area.

The improvements suggested here would not effect a major change overnight in Latin American attitudes; no grandiose plan nor magic formula is offered. Yet the suggestions would probably go far toward keeping the southern republics ideologically on the side of the United States. The main point is not to take Latin American opinion for granted. Ideological affinity seems to be an unusually important objective in this region of the world, since at least in the near future, the purely military and strategic problems do not loom so large as in other areas. If there should be a prolonged relaxation of tensions between the opposing sides in the cold war, Latin Americans might well tend to become increasingly indifferent toward the United States and their nationalism assume increasingly an anti-Yankee slant. Skilled American diplomacy and enlightened economic policies are of course prerequisite to good relations with Latin America; the most subtle propaganda is no real substitute. On the other hand, in the absence of an intelligent information and cultural program, economic and political policies can lose much of their effectiveness, can even backfire. The United States has the talent to contribute, and the financial expenditure need not be high, especially in comparison with military and economic aid programs elsewhere.

We have now completed our study of the broad and complex framework of United States-Latin American relations as a whole, with particular concentration on the most important political, economic, and ideological problems and on proposed methods of solving them. In our final chapter we shall offer some reflections as to the probable course Latin American policy will take in the foreseeable future. In order to make these reflections more fruitful, we shall first undertake a few case studies of recent relations with specific Latin American countries. Each of these cases exemplifies a different concatenation of circumstances and interactions; each has posed problems of a high order for American foreign-policy architects.

-IX-

Guatemala: Dilemma and Responsibility

Beyond question the most startling development in postwar inter-American relations has been the crisis in Guatemala. For the first time in history a Communist-oriented government gained control of a Latin American country, and the United States found itself faced with the unenviable task of having to get rid of that regime, *without violating its nonintervention pledge.* In contrast to its procedure in Bolivia, the United States had allowed conditions to deteriorate to the point where drastic American action unfortunately became mandatory. This action has undeniably done at least some damage to inter-American relations, though there are widely varying estimates as to how much. Just as in Bolivia, the United States now has a continuing commitment in Guatemala.

Guatemala, about the size of Tennessee, is located between Mexico to the north and El Salvador and Honduras to the south and east. The population of 2,800,000 is about 65 per cent Indian (Mayan-descent), 30 per cent mestizo (called *Ladino* in Guatemala), and the rest white or largely white: a population distribution roughly the same as that in Bolivia. Seventy-five per cent of the people are illiterate. As in Bolivia, the effective political, economic, and psychological nerve center of the nation, Guatemala City, is the plateau city. Guatemala's terrain is mountainous but not so formidable as to make economic integration of the country as difficult as it is in Bolivia. In fact, Guatemala has had for some time a comparatively prosperous economy, dependent primarily upon the export of coffee (82 per cent of total value of exports) and bananas to the United States. The only industries of any consequence—all American-owned—are the United Fruit Company plantations, the International Railways of Central America system, and the Electric Power Company (Empresa Eléctrica).

134

Though the economy has been prosperous, the mass of the people have lived under conditions of poverty. Most of them have earned about forty cents a day on the coffee plantations; in contrast, the Fruit Company has paid its employees about $2.00 a day. About 3 per cent of the population has owned about 70 per cent of the land, although much good land is still available for distribution. In 1950, only 163 persons owned 41 per cent of the cultivated farm acreage.

Until 1944 Guatemala had a plentiful share of dictators and repressive regimes that culminated in the dictatorship of General Jorge Ubico (1932-1944). The Fruit Company and the railway system introduced an economic stimulus around 1900. Though a small middle class gradually appeared, only its urban commercial elements and the few who managed to obtain middle-ranking positions with the American concerns gained any real benefit from the new status. In particular, frustrated intellectuals, schoolteachers, and labor leaders became an easy prey to "isms." During World War II, younger army officers who trained at military installations in the United States became distressed with the retarded conditions in their country when they returned. During this period a definite trend toward nationalism appeared for the first time—paralleling the National Revolutionary Movement (MNR) trend in Bolivia after the Chaco War—along with pressures for greater economic and social equality.

Missing was a formula for a new and arresting synthesis. It was supplied by the Marxian dialectic, which explained that Guatemala was an economic colony, exploited partly by its "reactionary" domestic landlord class, but primarily by the "economic imperialism" of the American-owned Fruit Company. This type of thinking was stimulated by labor leaders and by contacts with Vicente Lombardo Toledano, the pro-Communist Mexican labor leader, and political exiles in meetings with radical circles in Chile, Argentina, and France. Allied wartime propaganda and the statements in the Atlantic Charter helped intensify the new attitudes.

In 1944 the Ubico dictatorship was overthrown by a combination consisting largely of young army officers, schoolteachers, and

135

labor leaders. Nationalism was the principal tie binding these groups. Two important, genuinely motivated reforms were introduced by the so-called "revolution of 1944," under the leadership of President Juan José Arévalo, a former schoolteacher himself. Teachers received definite economic benefits, and the dignity of the teaching profession itself was enhanced. Urban labor obtained the right to organize, to strike, and to receive compulsory preferential employment rights over foreigners. Social security coverage was expanded to cover both these groups. As education spread to the middle- and lower-middle-income groups, and these elements gained in station, they became open to newer and more radical ideas. Nor was any effort made at this early stage to introduce agrarian reform.

Thus, a leftist, progressive, but non-Communist government directed the fortunes of Guatemala in the early revolutionary stages. Unfortunately Kremlin-directed Communists took the helm. If ever there was a classic example of Communist victory by default, Guatemala provided it. In the early years under President Arévalo there was considerable opposition to the Communists, but it was rendered ineffective, primarily by the Communists' aggressive support of the objectives of the 1944 revolution and by their political warfare tactics. Arévalo found himself increasingly, though not totally, dependent upon Communist political and administrative support. With the election of President Jacobo Arbenz in 1950, the Communists were able to achieve the thinly disguised domination of the Guatemalan government which they had been seeking.

Furthermore, their espousal of the popular agrarian reform law of 1952 added to their political strength and influence. Actually Guatemala did not need "agrarian reform" in the same sense as did Mexico and Bolivia. Unlike the situation in those countries, a substantial amount of good land belonging to the government was still available for distribution, including the expropriated German *fincas*. Even under Ubico an effort had been made to give land to many of the peasants, but they evinced general apathy; and no Guatemalan peasant leader like Emiliano Zapata of Mexico, no grass-roots movement, arose in answer. The reform was forced by the Communist-dominated government, and Communists administered the agrarian committees that distributed the land, thus receiving the credit. By the time of the anti-Communist revolt in 1954, the distribution had proceeded rapidly only in the province of Escuintla, where the Communist-dominated committees agitated the restless *Ladinos,* inciting them to seize properties. It is essential to note that the peasants received the land not in fee simple but rather on a rental basis, with the government becoming the actual owner. Had "reform" proceeded much longer in this fashion, the Communists, following the example of Mao Tse-Tung's "Yenan Way," would have built up a peasant base in addition to their urban labor one.

The strategy and tactics of the Communists were clearly dictated by the Kremlin. The key leaders—Manuel Fortuny, secretary general of the Communist Party (disguised as the "Labor Party"), Víctor Gutiérrez, head of the Labor Commission, and Carlos Pellecer, the agrarian leader—had with others made trips to Iron Curtain countries, where they received their instructions. By 1954 though they had only four members in the 56-man congress, the Communists, through second- and third-level positions, dominated the presidency, the labor ministry and social security administration, the agrarian department, and the government press, radio, and propaganda unit.

The army, key to political overturn in Guatemala, had been "buttered up" by Arbenz to the point where it was benevolently neutral, though sympathetic to any group which would further the popular objectives of the movement of 1944. Only toward the end did certain important groups in the higher echelons of the army become alarmed at the increasing Communist influence. That their loyalty to the Arbenz administration was not very deep was evidenced by their refusal to fight against the rebels when the time came.

The tragedy of the opposition was that its two main components were sharply divided. No Bolivian *MNR* dynamism, no man of the stature of Paz Estenssoro, could be found to challenge the Communists. The enlightened liberals in Guatemala City supported

137

the objectives of 1944, but were against the seizure of the movement by international Communism. In contrast, the largely absentee
landowning class remained generally aloof from politics and based
their opposition to the Communists on purely selfish grounds. "A
Communist is anybody who wants what you've got," was their
motto. They had very little understanding of the social changes
taking place in Guatemala. The Catholic Church, understaffed
and lacking any vigorous interest in social reforms, had little
influence in the situation. Much later, toward the end of the whole
period, a pastoral letter of Archbishop Rossell Arellano of Guatemala condemned the Communist domination. In fairness, it
should be repeated that the Church has attempted to eschew
active involvement in politics, in view of the anticlericalism of
and previous friction with the state. By 1954 the Communist-
oriented regime had become increasingly unpopular because of
its brutally repressive methods, and little mass effort defended it
against the rebels. Nevertheless it is significant that the actual
initiative to overthrow the regime originated with exiled military
officers outside the country. The Communists had effectively used
a combination of the "carrot and the stick."

American policy toward the developing crisis in Guatemala
might best be characterized by a cartoon on the Nicaragua-Costa
Rican dispute that appeared (as late as 1955) in a highly respected
American newspaper. It showed a boy attempting to do his serious "homework" on the Formosan situation while the Central
American "bee" distractingly buzzed around him. Only a few
people in the United States were aware that the Communists were
increasing their strength in Guatemala, and even fewer considered
the Central American situation a major problem.

Our ambassador to Guatemala in the earlier part of the Arévalo
regime, Edwin J. Kyle, had been friendly to Arévalo and unaware
of the sinister influences at work, though in fairness to him it should
be said that few Americans were aware of Communist growth at
that time. In 1947 occurred the first real evidence of Yankee concern. The American Federation of Labor, which had become
increasingly aware of Communist efforts to gain control of the

labor movement, sent its Latin American representative, Serafino Romualdi, to Guatemala to help build up the non-Communist railway labor leadership. The Communists blocked his efforts, however, and from then on gained increasing dominance. The next ambassador, Richard C. Patterson, Jr., collided with Arévalo in 1948-1949 on the labor courts' partiality in ruling against a United Fruit Company strike. Patterson erred in allowing the official representative of the United States to be identified with the interests of the Fruit Company. Arévalo is reported to have referred to the "United States Fruit Company." Patterson was generally rather blunt in his statements and dealings with the sensitive Latins, much in the manner of Spruille Braden in Argentina. He perceived that sinister influences were at work, but he antagonized too many people and had to be recalled.

His successor, Rudolph E. Schoenfeld, was an experienced career diplomat, brilliant and alert to Communist strategy and tactics, especially after an assignment in Ana Pauker's Rumania. His appointment to Guatemala coincided with the beginning of Arbenz' term in 1951 and the virulent emergence of the Communists. Completely aware of what was going on, he kept Washington thoroughly briefed but was not cast in the role of a "man of action."

Meanwhile, high-level government officials in Washington continued to give little thought to Guatemala. Busy containing or counteracting Communist aggression in places like France, Italy, Iran, Korea, and Indo-China, they found it hard to become greatly concerned about its presence in a small "banana republic" far from the centers of Communist power. Senator Henry Cabot Lodge, Jr., of Massachusetts, had spoken out earlier about the Communist menace in Guatemala, but Congress paid little attention to it after that. As late as January, 1954, practically the only voices heard were those of Lodge and of Senator Alexander Wiley of Wisconsin.

Nor did the general American public know much about the situation. A handful of publications, notably the *New York Times,* the *Christian Science Monitor,* and *Time,* did keep track of developments, but their total impact was hardly significant. One statement, made on October 14, 1953, by a high government official,

139

caught the public eye: John Moors Cabot, assistant secretary for Inter-American Affairs, warned that Guatemala was now "openly playing the Communist game."

In November, 1953, a decisive turning point came in American policy toward Guatemala. It became evident that the Communist venom inexorably would continue to permeate the body politic of Guatemala, and there seemed to be no way of halting the process short of drastic action. The dilemma was essentially this: How could the United States tactfully win the support of the other hemispheric nations to eliminate on a *multilateral* basis this Communist threat to their security and common welfare? First, a meeting must be held at which international Communism would be singled out, apart from other totalitarianisms, as a threat to the security of the hemisphere; second, each of the Latin American nations must be informed of the extent of Communist penetration of Guatemala, a job which had until then been done inadequately; third, consultation should be taken on specific joint measures. A final, though unwelcome, eventuality could not be overlooked. The United States must stand ready, if necessary, to intervene unilaterally, or perhaps with the aid of only a few Latin American nations. This last possibility was obviously distasteful and would have to be a dangerously calculated risk. Yet which was the lesser of two evils: to cause a wave of anti-Yankeeism to sweep most of Latin America, or to allow a strategic Soviet politico-ideological base to come into existence in Latin America? Fortunately the United States was not driven to this extreme, but it came close to it.

The principal man of action was Ambassador John E. Peurifoy, though Secretary John Foster Dulles and Assistant Secretary for Inter-American Affairs Henry Holland were also to play significant roles, and a number of Latin American policy men in the State Department "burned the midnight oil" at their desks during the weeks when the Guatemalan crisis was at its critical phase. Ambassador Peurifoy was transferred in November, 1953, from Greece, where he had played a decisive anti-Communist role. He was energetic, jaunty, and obviously knowledgeable about fighting Communists. But Guatemala was no Greece. For one thing, the

140

small Central American country had a more volatile political atmosphere, and it was therefore harder to predict the course of events. The new ambassador soon discovered that at this late date to entertain hopes of splitting the genuine nationalists from the Communists was to indulge in wishful thinking.

During the next few months various rumors circulated that a boycott might be imposed on Guatemala. It was alleged that drastic reductions in American imports of coffee, Guatemala's principal source of foreign exchange, or curtailment of petroleum shipments (Guatemala produces none and customarily has only a few days' supply on hand) would soon cause the Communist-dominated regime to topple. Apart from the technical difficulties involved, any such actions would become publicly known and would unquestionably bring down upon the United States the condemnation of most of Latin America, and perhaps of the world. Besides, application of a coffee boycott would hurt primarily the very class, which, though completely ineffective, was strongly anti-Communist —the coffee planters. There is no available evidence that the United States government ever seriously considered trying these tactics.

With unilateral intervention and economic measures clearly ruled out, multilateral consultation in the time-honored inter-American way seemed the only recourse. At an Inter-American Conference held at Caracas in March, 1954, a declaration was passed condemning the domination or control of the political institutions of any American state by the international Communist movement, and calling for international policing measures and exchange of information concerning Communist activities. Guatemala was not mentioned.

The Caracas declaration passed—but with difficulty, for three reasons. In the first place, many Latin Americans have tended consistently to feel that the Soviets have no serious designs in far-off Latin America. While recognizing that Latin American Communists do receive ideological and material sustenance from behind the Iron Curtain, they regard Communists as primarily local radicals who can always be kept under control when necessary. Secondly, the Latin Americans, acutely conscious now of being "under-

141

developed," are primarily concerned with economic development and social progress. They appeared to regard the anti-Communist resolution as a chore to be taken care of with dispatch, in order to get to the really important business of any inter-American meeting— economic matters. Some nations, like Uruguay, expressed the conviction that Communism can best be defeated through economic and social progress. Last, but by no means least, the Latin American nations feared that an anti-Communist resolution might be abused to allow Yankee intervention in the internal affairs of any Latin American country, which was more feared by them than the Communist threat. Consequently, a solid vote for the declaration was not presented at Caracas. Guatemala naturally voted against the declaration; and two important countries, Argentina and Mexico, abstained, so that the vote was 17–1. Furthermore, certain other countries later expressed their misgivings at having voted in the affirmative.

Guatemala's foreign minister, Guillermo Toriello, played effectively upon Latin fears of Yankee intervention when he declared with eloquence:

. . . They have counseled boycott and economic aggression against Guatemala in the press and even from parliamentary tribunes. Still not content and seeing the failure of all their efforts, now again invoking the sacred word, democracy, and repeating the absurd pretext that Guatemala is a "beachhead of Communism in America," and that the small republic constitutes a threat to the security of an entire continent, they dare to commit the ultimate attempt, now no longer against Guatemala alone, but against the most solid structure of Pan-Americanism, in proposing active intervention against the Guatemalan government.

In the course of this speech Toriello raised the naive question as to what exactly was meant by international Communism and how did it constitute a threat. Despite Secretary Dulles' subsequent assault upon this vulnerable point, Toriello's emotional oratory unquestionably had more influence than Dulles' speech upon many of the Latin delegates. One of his most effective points concerned

Guatemala's relations with the United Fruit Company. He maintained that "semi-colonial" Guatemala was simply attempting to "liberate" the country from foreign economic interests. Specifically, it was building a highway to the Pacific to rival the Fruit Company-owned railway system, and was expanding national ports and docks to allow for foreign trade other than that carried by the Fruit Company's White Fleet. With the agrarian reform, the Arbenz regime was "abolishing the latifundia, including those of the United Fruit Company itself." An attempt was also being made to end the virtual foreign monopoly of electric power. All these statements were well calculated to arouse the deepest sympathy of many of the other Latin American delegates, since they too represented countries with some of the same nationalistic urges and resentments as Guatemala's.

Thus the Caracas conference ended on a note of questionable triumph for those who were anxious to see the defeat of Communism in Guatemala. Indeed, in the eyes of many Latins Arbenz was guilty of only some distortion when he declared:

Some of the legal positions maintained by us were defeated but Caracas constituted a victory for our delegation, because it defeated the forces of imperialism and feudalism that raised the banner of anti-Communism in order to intervene in the affairs of the Latin American nations.

On May Day Arbenz scornfully proclaimed that the United Fruit Company, after exploiting Guatemala and exhausting many of its best lands, now had the audacity to demand payment for being unjustly treated. He was referring to the expropriation claim of $16 million which the State Department had presented to the Guatemalan government only two weeks earlier. In 1953 the Arbenz regime expropriated 239,624 acres of Fruit Company property, and in 1954 an additional 173,949, making a total of 413,573 acres. This left the company with about 150,000. The expropriation was unsuccessfully appealed, and Guatemala agreed to pay only $594,572 in agrarian bonds maturing in twenty-five years, with interest at 3 per cent. The company refused to accept

143

this settlement, and sought aid from the State Department, which, after studying the matter, asked that "prompt, adequate and effective compensation" be made, pursuant to the principle established by Secretary Hull in the late 1930's in the dispute between Mexico and the oil companies. With no settlement forthcoming by February, 1954, the United States suggested that the case be taken to the Court of Arbitration at The Hague (as provided for in the Fruit Company's 1936 contract). Guatemala rejected this solution, whereupon the United States asked for a payment of about $16 million in compensation.

This sequence of events has been spelled out because relations between Guatemala and the United Fruit Company appear to have been an "Achilles' heel" for anti-American propaganda. The United States government, as previously in Mexico, never questioned the sovereign right of Guatemala to expropriate; it merely maintained that the price for the acreage involved was inadequate compensation and expressed its willingness to have the matter arbitrated. It is also well to keep in mind that Guatemala, with its abundant dollar coffee exports, was in a much better financial situation than Mexico or Bolivia had been to pay adequate remuneration. Its later purchase of Iron Curtain armaments was to prove this. The Arbenz government treated this issue not as a matter of international diplomacy or economic relations but as a theme for propaganda.

This is not to say that the Fruit Company's record in Guatemala was entirely spotless. There are apparently three ways in which the company might be open to criticism. First, it could have renegotiated its contract under the Arévalo regime, when there was a chance of getting a fair deal. It might thereby have given Guatemala a larger share of the profits, as it later did in Costa Rica and has even more recently done under the new Guatemalan regime. Secondly, during the big strike of 1948-1949 and on a few later occasions, the company might well have displayed less resistance toward legitimate labor demands and thereby avoided making the workers susceptible to Communist propaganda and influence. Thirdly, the company could have divested itself earlier

144

of its controlling interest in the railway system of Guatemala, thus making it a less vulnerable target for ultranationalist and Communist appeals. An independent close observer of the Guatemalan scene during several years' residence there maintains that the role of the Fruit Company in the economic life of the nation has been greatly exaggerated. It actually employs only a small labor force in proportion to the total number of the gainfully employed, and its plantations occupy only a tiny part of the cultivable land. While most of the well-educated Guatemalans in the capital vaguely dislike the Fruit Company, they really know little about its banana operations and have no specific complaints to make about them. What has caused considerable ill feeling is the allegedly poor service and discriminatory rates of the railway, from Guatemala City to Puerto Barrios on the coast, which is controlled by the company. According to the same observer, the allegedly bad service and high rates charged by the local light and power company add fuel to the fire.

In recent years, the Fruit Company has carried out generally enlightened, progressive policies, including on the whole good treatment of its labor, establishment of agricultural schools and hospitals, and provision to send Guatemalans and other Central Americans to the United States on fellowships. Yet its less attractive heritage lingers on. Despite great efforts by its public-relations department, the general public, both north and south, feels that it is not a progressive company. One trouble is that no thorough work by an independent, competent, unprejudiced observer is available for its operations in recent years. It is hoped that publication of the National Planning Association's Case Study on the Company, now under way, will go far toward filling this gap.

In 1954, then, upon the general impasse in United States-Guatemalan relations, one of those fortuitous events that reveal a path toward solution of thorny international problems occurred. In retrospect, one wonders how a resolution of the dilemma could otherwise have been found, so well entrenched were the Communists, and so sympathetic were many of the Latin American countries to the Guatemalan stand on foreign intervention. Briefly,

145

the Arbenz regime overreached itself. Guatemala was concerned over United States arms shipments to Guatemala's neighbors under standard military assistance pacts, and was unable itself to purchase arms this side of the Iron Curtain. The Arbenz regime therefore purchased from behind the Iron Curtain and received in May, 1954, 2,000 tons of armaments valued at $10 million (one-sixth of Guatemala's entire budget), which made it the most heavily armed state in Central America.

This flagrant act served at last to awaken the majority of Latin American countries to the fact that Guatemala did indeed have close connections with international Communism. Furthermore, it particularly alarmed Guatemala's neighbors, and Nicaragua issued a call under the Rio defense treaty for a meeting of Inter-American foreign ministers to preserve Central America from a threat to its peace and security. The United States stopped some vessels in the Caribbean suspected of carrying arms to Guatemala and asked its European friends for permission to block all such traffic. To many European nations, however, the request seemed to infringe upon their right to peacetime freedom of the seas. The Arbenz regime finally took fright and offered to sign a nonagression pact with Honduras and to settle the Fruit Company issue with Ambassador Peurifoy. Apart from the question of the arms, Honduras was not friendly to Guatemala at this time, because responsibility for certain labor strikes on its Fruit Company plantations had been placed unmistakably on Communist agitators trained in Guatemala. As for the Fruit Company issue, Peurifoy made it quite clear that Communists were the real problem. He said that he would be glad to discuss the Communist issue but would merely act as a transfer agent for the company. This attitude was sharply different from the one which Ambassador Patterson had adopted. Reinforcing Peurifoy's stand was the following flat statement by a State Department official:

If the Guatemalans paid the United Fruit Company's full $16,000,000 claim tomorrow and decorated every last United Fruit official with the Order of the Quetzal, we wouldn't be one whit less concerned with the danger of Communism in Guatemala.

146

In the light of Nicaragua's call for a meeting, the United States at long last circularized the Latin American foreign ministries with detailed information on Communist activities in Guatemala. It stressed that it was not seeking economic sanctions but rather an anti-Communist resolution with some teeth in it, an embargo on arms to Guatemala, and the establishment of a five-nation commission to watch carefully developments in Guatemala. By the middle of June, every nation had agreed to attend a meeting on July 5. What would have happened at such a meeting will never be known, since on June 18 a successful anti-Communist revolt was launched from Honduras by Colonel Carlos Castillo Armas. But note that a *multilateral* meeting was scheduled to be held to solve the Guatemalan problem; many critics either willfully or in ignorance disregard this fact.

During the next nine days the Guatemalan case was in the headlines of the world's newspapers. Latin America received more news coverage during that period than it had in many years. Soviet foreign broadcasts, which had for some time devoted a comparatively large amount of attention to Guatemala, reached a peak of thirty-five broadcasts in one day. Furthermore, Guatemala provided the United Nations with an interesting and provocative test case. As far as the United States was concerned, the essential objective was to keep the United Nations Security Council and the Soviet Union out of hemispheric affairs, and to build up the prestige of the OAS by allowing it to handle this case, properly within its sphere. At this point the Guatemalan situation moved out of a purely local realm and became hemispheric and even global in its ramifications; as such it has been described in Chapter V, above.

Did the United States government or private American interests render military aid to the rebels? If so, this would have been the most flagrant kind of intervention—a "Panama case" all over again, even if directed against Communists. No evidence appears to indicate that either public or private United States interests did aid the rebellion. It is highly unlikely that, apart from other considerations, the Fruit Company would have taken the great risk of allowing itself in these times to become directly involved in a military overturn. Yet, many people, including a number of Latin Americans, continue to believe that the United States gave military and financial assistance to the rebels. For a short while during and after the revolt, a wave of anti-Yankeeism swept most of Latin America, especially among students and intellectuals. Turbulent demonstrations occurred before American embassies, and the American flag was burned. However, this violent sentiment appeared to wane rapidly. How much anti-Yankee undercurrent has been left is difficult to estimate.

What is evident is that the United States did exercise unusually strong political influence, just as it later did economically and ideologically, to help the new regime. The statements of Ambassador Peurifoy and of spokesmen in Washington made it clear that the United States was opposed to the Arbenz regime and would look with sympathy on any anti-Communist group which would replace it. Certainly Castillo Armas could read the signs of encouragement and he did so. Furthermore, Ambassador Peurifoy played a key role in arranging for the succession to the Arbenz regime (perhaps with more publicity than prudence). He refused to agree to the assumption of power by General Díaz, who was favorable to the Communists, and flew to San Salvador to aid in effecting a compromise between the two leading candidates for head of the new anti-Communist military junta. Let it be emphasized, however, that his advice and intercession were requested. At any rate, it is obvious that the role of the American ambassador in a small Central American country cannot help being a highly influential one.

Now, had the United States intervened unilaterally in Guatemala's affairs? It will be recalled that our definition of Yankee intervention is: direct interposition of military force, or diplomatic or economic sanctions by the United States alone in a Latin American country. The United States did not militarily aid the revolutionaries, but did any of its other actions come under this definition? Three aspects merit examination: the statements of Ambassador Peurifoy and of spokesmen in Washington in open opposition to the Arbenz regime; the generally highhanded manner in which Peurifoy conducted himself; and his statement to General Díaz that the United States would not recognize a regime headed by Díaz, because of continuing Communist direction. Without pronouncing a final verdict on the question, one can only say that if these three moves did not constitute diplomatic intervention, they at least came dangerously close. It would not take a strong Yankeephobe, even necessarily a Latin nationalist, to call the moves unequivocally Yankee intervention. Unquestionably the objective sought was laudable—to rid the Americas of a hostile, Communist-oriented regime. But what is suggested here is that the manner in which the objective was accomplished was one that did little good for United States-Latin American relations.

Leaving this stage of the Guatemalan dilemma, we now turn to a new phase of American responsibility, one which also has pitfalls. The new president, Colonel Castillo Armas, was an honest, courageous military man and a fairly able administrator, but not a leader of the stature of Bolivia's President Paz Estenssoro or Siles Zuazo. He had not devoted his life to the study of complex economic and social problems, nor did he have a well-organized political and ideological base to support him, as the Bolivians have in the National Revolutionary Movement (MNR) party. The problems which the new Guatemalan president had to face were formidable indeed, greater than those confronting the MNR regime.

Though Guatemala's general foreign and domestic economic conditions were not in the severe straits that those of Bolivia were, the political and financial situations of the new regime, and the morale in the vital labor movement and teaching profession, were far worse. After restoring political law' and order, Castillo Armas jailed hundreds of Communists and pro-Communist leaders, dissolved all leftist political parties, and suppressed any evidences of Communist activity. He managed to establish an understanding with the army, which had not resisted his rebel forces, but which still remained largely sympathetic to the previous regime. Meanwhile the numerous ultraconservatives were clustering around the landowning class, who seemed to have "learned nothing and forgotten nothing." Castillo Armas' political course might be

149

described as a passage between the Scylla of mild leftism on the part of the army and the Charybdis of extreme rightism on the part of the powerful conservative groups in the country. Such an analysis would put the new president slightly "right of center," which seems a good way to describe his personal outlook. Still, he did not appear to have any definite political philosophy of his own, nor the backing of any well-organized political party.

Through 1956 Castillo Armas continued to rule as the usual "strong man." By requiring voters to be literate, he has disenfranchised 75 per cent of the people. This may be understandable as a temporary measure, since the illiterate peasants blindly voted as the Communist-oriented regime directed them and could be manipulated by any other government. If not accompanied by positive measures to increase literacy, however, it will obviously be a retrogressive measure in the long run. Some schools have been constructed and hospitals improved, but only a start has been made.

Wisely, the agrarian reform measures were not reversed immediately. Instead, 55,000 of the 87,000 families who had received rights to land under the Arbenz regime now received them in fee simple, thus making them genuine proprietors and not simply government wards, as they had been. But many families who had illegally seized land were dispossessed by the landowners and by the government, though first the agrarian bonds had to be surrendered to the government and the peasants allowed to harvest their crops. Also many "squatters" fled of their own volition. Among the lands returned were about 200,000 acres given back to the United Fruit Company. In March, 1956, a new statute was passed, according to which 25,000 families would be resettled over a five-year period on some of the 330,000 acres of good unused national land in the northern Reyna province. The tracts would be deeded in fee simple to the entire family, not just its head. They would be frozen against mortgage or attachment, since the original owners must keep them at least twenty-five years, and could then be sold only with the consent of the entire family. The objective was to disperse thousands of national acres in orderly fashion, rather than to divide the large commercially profitable private estates.

150

Private lands which were expropriated would be paid for in legal tender, over a ten-year period, at 4 per cent interest, as compared to the former system of twenty-five-year, 3 per cent agrarian bonds. Property owners would have one year to cultivate good land, and two for bad land. This differed sharply from the procedure under the Arbenz government, whereby the property was expropriated immediately upon declaration by the government that it had purposely been left fallow. Finally, the Castillo Armas government instituted a new sliding-scale tax on uncultivated land, with an increase of 25 per cent each year.

The agrarian policy of the regime, then, was to create a nation of independent, secure property owners, large and small. No further drastic expropriations were to take place, as unused national lands were to be made available. However, by the judicious use of gradual expropriation and taxation devices, an increase in agricultural productivity would be fostered. Many of these measures made landowners and peasants unhappy and were a cause of political uncertainty and unrest in the provinces.

Castillo Armas has characterized his program as one aiming at "social justice, sustenance, education, employment, improved economy, and respect for the human being." In addition to political backing, this program requires funds. But the new president found the treasury deficit to be about $30 million, which the "progressive capitalists" of the Arbenz regime had stolen. He first asked for a voluntary donation of $1 million, but the landowning "fat cats" were unwilling to contribute any money to the regime which had saved them from the Communists. Angered by this refusal of support, Castillo Armas imposed a forced levy of $6,200,000, involving 3 per cent of the value of real property over $5,000, 1 per cent of business capital over $5,000, 10 per cent of the average monthly earnings of professional men, and lump-sum payments of $10,000 from large sugar mills. Thus this "one shot" tax was equitably distributed. Nevertheless, it is evident that Castillo Armas has not received the financial and moral support which he merits. Consequently he has encouraged foreign investments, especially in petroleum development. A return of the

$50 million in "flight capital" which had been invested abroad
would be a great asset to the financial situation. The fluctuation
price of Guatemala's principal export, coffee, is a timely reminder
that the country should seek to diversify its economy to some extent.

Unfortunately, toward the end of 1956, there were ominous signs
that Castillo Armas, finding both left- and right-wing opposition
to his efforts, was beginning to revert to what could only be termed
unenlightened strong-arm methods. Opponents were crushed under
the slogan of anti-Communism. The peasants, dispossessed of
the land they had occupied, were unhappy. Trade unions, smashed
in the revolution, had been allowed to make only a slight comeback.
A thirty-day state of siege, third-degree methods, reminiscent of
Communist days, and corruption at high levels of the government
were the order of the day. Certain "middle-of-the roaders," non-
Communist leftists, intellectuals, and the always vociferous but
volatile students were the chief opposition to the regime, and the
large landowners were doing little to help it. Taking advantage
of this disaffection was an organized Red underground. The problem was how to control the Communists without repressing all
dissent. A government spokesman said, "Ours is the party of force,
combat and of organized violence—if our enemies ask for it." If
this was all the Castillo Armas regime had to offer, the outlook
was a bleak one indeed.

What has the United States done to help Guatemala recuperate
and achieve progress? At first, the words of its officials seemed
much more impressive than their deeds. Secretary Dulles publicly
announced that the United States would help Guatemala become
"prosperous and progressive" in order to "alleviate the conditions"
which gave rise to Communism. For several months afterwards,
however, the only concrete aid was $40,000 in medical supplies.
After a Congressional airing, $6,400,000 in Point Four technical
assistance was extended immediately to Guatemala, and in the
fiscal year 1955-1956, $15 million in aid was extended, of which
$2,400,000 was earmarked to help resettle the 25,000 farm families.
Actual implementation of the technical assistance program has been
greatly delayed. In fairness to American governmental adminis-

trators, it should be said that it is not always easy to find quickly an effective way of putting to use a large sum of money in an underdeveloped country. The Castillo Armas regime has not thus far revealed a high level of administrative capacity in drawing up practical projects. Since some disillusionment and anti-American sentiment are already evident in Guatemala, however, more expeditious handling of American assistance seems vital.

The extension of a World Bank loan for highway development has greatly aided Guatemala. Both Atlantic and Pacific branches will be built. In particular, completion of the contemplated 190-mile all-weather road from Guatemala City to the coast will mean that at last Guatemala will no longer be exclusively dependent on the Fruit Company-controlled railway for transportation between its capital city and the ocean.

Meanwhile, the United Fruit Company has finally renegotiated its contract to allow the Guatemalan government to obtain 30 per cent of the company's profits, on the pattern of its Costa Rican agreement. It has also turned over 120,000 acres of land which it does not need. The company should encourage even more than it has the growth of a free and healthy trade-unionism on its plantations, not so easy an objective to attain as many suppose. The company might also upgrade some of the more promising Guatemalan employees to executive positions. For some time, as we have seen, it has been carrying out a "Point Four" program of its own. Like any company it must show profits to its stockholders, but such measures might well in the end work to its advantage.

It is difficult to estimate the economic effects of the antitrust suit brought by the United States government against the company. Politically, it has caused a favorable reaction throughout most of Latin America, but it would seem best for American interests not to let this drag on interminably; perhaps a consent decree may be obtained, indicating that the policies alleged in the suit are no longer being practiced. If the International Railways of Central America and the Empresa Eléctrica could come to a mutually satisfactory agreement with the Guatemalan government about the degree and form of governmental control over service and rates, this would undoubtedly improve their services and create better will.

Fortunately our foreign-policy officials have understood that economic aid is not enough. It is essential to refurbish the Guatemalan labor movement with the leadership of which it has been stripped, and to drain the Communist poison from the minds of the nation's teachers, who mold the minds of Guatemalan youth. The AFL-CIO and Rutgers University sent their Latin American labor experts to Guatemala to advise and aid the weak leadership of the new labor movement. Approximately one hundred teachers were invited for two-month stays in the southwestern United States (at an expense to the United States of only $170,000), where they were taught American public-school methods. All this aid was extended by the United States on the basis of requests by the Guatemalan government, although suggestions were properly made by United States officials as to what aid was available. Finally, the appointment of Norman Armour as ambassador to Guatemala meant that the United States temporarily had in this critical post its most distinguished and experienced Latin American diplomat. Armour knew well how to advise and influence, without interfering excessively. The present (1956) ambassador, Edward J. Sparks, brings to his Guatemalan post valuable experience gained in Bolivia.

Meanwhile two blasts against the United States have emanated from Mexico in the aftermath of the Guatemalan revolt, neither of which can be dismissed completely. While in Mexico, former President Arbenz, on his way to become a Swiss citizen, accused the United States of financing with millions of dollars Castillo Armas and his band of mercenaries and adventurers. He warned that American "imperialism" would gradually subjugate all of Latin America. Diego Rivera, the famous Mexican Communist artist, painted a picture in which he showed all of the "devilish" people responsible for the Guatemalan overturn. In the picture, a rat-faced Castillo Armas, who has a thick packet of $10,000 bills, shakes hands with Secretary Dulles; Dulles' brother, Allen,

154

head of Central Intelligence, whispers in the Secretary's ear. The Secretary, clad in a paratrooper's uniform, grips an H-bomb, on which appears a leering caricature of President Eisenhower. Ambassador Peurifoy hands out dollar bills to Guatemalan soldiers. Downtrodden workers load a banana boat; the corpses of little children lie disregarded underfoot. The papal nuncio blesses the joyous scene. How many non-Communist Latin Americans may be influenced by these blasts, in view of their sources, is debatable, but the seeds of suspicion are already sown, and propaganda items like these can be potent, especially at any future times of stress in United States-Latin American relations.

Thus we come to the end of the Guatemalan story. What is the real significance of Guatemala for the foreign relations of the United States? In the first place, it seems clear that a complete Soviet triumph in Guatemala would have been a political or ideological defeat of major proportions for the United States. That the Soviet Union could capture a country far removed from the Red Army (unlike Czechoslovakia, for example), in the midst of the American sphere of influence, would have added to its prestige and hurt that of the United States everywhere. Furthermore, the Communists would have gained valuable experience on how to adapt themselves, chameleon-like, to conditions in an underdeveloped country, and how to extend their influence from the captive base to neighboring underdeveloped countries. This last point merits emphasis. The small country of Guatemala was not the real Soviet target; rather it was to gain a foothold somewhere in the New World, from which Communism could extend throughout the rest of the hemisphere. Whether the Communists governed the country overtly or dominated it through a façade, as in Guatemala, was irrelevant as far as achievement of their basic objectives was concerned. Even in the face of their apparent failure, the Communists did succeed in inciting the United States to make moves which looked very much like intervention.

Secondly, in contrast to its Bolivian performance, the United States allowed the largely genuine nationalist revolution of 1944 in Guatemala to flounder almost unnoticed, thus making it easy

155

prey for the dynamic Communists. The Communists, though small in number, through the securing of a few strategic positions were able to dominate a country in Guatemala's early stage of development. Hopelessly divided into liberals and ultraconservatives, the opposition proved no match for the Communists, who moved in largely through default. A large American corporation proved to be an excellent scapegoat for ultranationalists and Communists, and a number of uninformed Americans tended largely to accept the version of these doctrinaire Yankeephobes on this aspect. The United States finally had to take drastic, unwelcome action. The whole affair pointed out that "it could happen here" in this hemisphere, that the United States should be on guard against its possible recurrence. It also revealed a great need to make quickly available accurate information concerning any similar future trend both to the American public and to Latin American, European, and other friendly powers. Naturally the timing of the release and the dissemination of this information would have to be done with great care. A badly timed "Blue Book" or "White Paper" on sinister conditions in any Latin American country might merely arouse nationalist opinion against the United States and aggravate those conditions. Ample prior consultation with Latin American foreign ministers would seem essential.

Finally, the United States learned that eradicating Communism was only half of the task. The new anti-Communist regime, largely inexperienced and lacking in able political leaders, must be encouraged to pursue progressive policies. It must not be allowed to lapse into an anachronistic dictatorship. The rest of Latin America is closely watching American policy toward Guatemala. There is no need for Yankees to apologize for having displayed firmness in combatting Communism in Guatemala, though the manner in which it was done is open to criticism. However, should a retrogressive situation develop, it will seem to many Latin Americans that the United States is concerned with negative anti-Communism and with protection of its big business interests, not with Latins' genuine desires for progress. Such a reaction would certainly be detrimental to American policy interests in this hemisphere. Thus the United States must continue to exert strong and direct influence in a Latin American country in order to bring about a situation which will improve its inter-American relations. This constructive use of its influence should not be termed Yankee intervention, according to our definition. A permanent reversion to repressive one-party dictatorship, or what people have labeled "banana reactionism," would be definitely harmful to American foreign-policy interests. Yet, Guatemala cannot be allowed to become a "poorhouse of quarreling inmates." Thus a firm hand is necessary. The American commitment continues in Guatemala under these difficult circumstances.

-X-

Bolivia: A Calculated Risk

Bolivia is an excellent illustration of the pattern of dictatorship combined with a trend toward strong nationalism and a potential threat of Communism. The country has alternated throughout much of its history between dictatorship and chaos. In recent years it has produced one of the most intense examples of genuine nationalism in Latin America. Furthermore, though Communist influence is not currently great, it is potentially strong. Out of this complex of factors has come the only genuine Latin American revolution other than the one in Mexico. The United States has found itself compelled to play an active role in this remote trouble spot, far removed from its immediate security interests. In formulating its policy toward Bolivia, the United States has been able to draw upon its Mexican experience, where it learned that a social revolution was taking place which was to change the character of its relations with that country. In Bolivia it was to learn that its influence had to be brought strongly to bear on the course of events.

Because the Bolivian case is less known to the American public than that of Guatemala, more space will be given in this chapter to the background of internal developments. Bolivia, twice the size of Spain and situated in the geographical center of South America, is a paradoxical country. Its abject poverty in the midst of enormous natural wealth suggests the "beggar seated on a chair of gold." The retarded economic development is due in part to the extremely mountainous terrain, with peaks over 20,000 feet above sea level—a condition which presents formidable obstacles to communications and surface transportation. Air travel is at a premium. The principal cities, including La Paz, the capital, and Cochabamba, a mining center, are located on the high, dry plateau (10,000 to 14,000 feet). The mountains drop precipitously to the eastern lowlands in the Santa Cruz region. Coffee, cocoa, tropical fruits, rubber, hardwoods, and petroleum (in the Chaco district) can all be cultivated or produced within Bolivia's boundaries. High in the mountains, where once gold and silver were mined for the Spanish conquistadores, tin, tungsten, and antimony are now the principal mineral treasures. But, the lack of surface transportation facilities between the high plateau and the Santa Cruz lowlands has unquestionably been a major deterrent to the development of that fertile agricultural region.

Until quite recently, Bolivian life has been relatively little touched by the currents of world trade and commerce. Isolated in its mountain fastnesses and torn by internal strife, the country has attracted few immigrants, with the result that its population of 4 million is largely composed of Indians (55 per cent) and people of mixed blood, or *cholos* (35 per cent). The United Nations technical mission to Bolivia estimated that from one-half to two-thirds of the total population still live practically outside the money economy, on a more or less self-sustaining agricultural basis.*

Soon after the discovery of tin about half a century ago, a number of mines, dependent upon both foreign capital and Indian labor, were opened. Thus, in addition to the original class of agriculturists, there arose a class of mine workers who lived and toiled under adverse conditions. Virtually none of the large profit obtained from the export of tin, tungsten, and other minerals was reinvested in the country. The Indian by and large remained isolated from the new developments and lacked the incentive and knowledge to change his deeply imbedded customs and habits. The agricultural surplus needed for further economic growth never arose, and the foreign exchange acquired from the export of minerals was largely absorbed by payments for the import of food and consumption products. Thus, Bolivia became an economy split between the trading and agricultural sectors, almost totally dependent for its foreign-exchange and governmental revenue on the world price of tin. This unhappy situation has caused continual sharp financial

Report on the United Nations Mission of Technical Assistance to Bolivia (New York, 1951), p. 106.

159

and monetary fluctuations. With the exception of some of the tin miners, the great majority of the Bolivian workers and peasants are politically immature and have been so conditioned by despotism and false promises of democracy that they have little or no interest in their government. Under the present revolutionary regime, however, this general attitude is changing.

The extreme instability which has characterized Bolivia's political evolution has been both a cause and result of its retarded economic and social development. Although President Andrés Santa Cruz (1829-1839) was an outstanding statesman and made Bolivia an important country in South American politics, the political situation deteriorated after his administration. A graphic description of the state of affairs in the country, given by a Chilean diplomat in the mid-nineteenth century, generally characterizes Bolivia's condition during much of its past history: "The imprint of the sword is everywhere and the prostration of industry, the poverty of the Exchequer, charitable institutions suspended, educational establishments closed, public offices in chaos, justice neglected, public officials unpaid and abuse rampant, all combine to condemn the administration."[*]

The United Nations technical mission to Bolivia, reporting in 1951, observed that while other nations with roughly similar political experiences had yet later managed somehow to find solutions to many of their problems, Bolivia had not.

Prospective or possible sources of investment capital will not fail to note that no legally elected Bolivian president has served out his term in the last quarter century; that there have been seven presidents and eight revolutions in the last ten years; that there have been sixteen ministers of labor in four years; that the Bolivian Development Corporation has had five complete changes of its directorate in the past six years of its existence; that there have been eight ministers of finance within eighteen months.[†]

---

[*]Quoted in Harold Osborne, *Bolivia: A Land Divided* (London, 1954), p. 57.
[†]*Report on the United Nations Mission of Technical Assistance to Bolivia*, p. 3.

As if this political heritage were not disastrous enough, history saw fit to inflict on Bolivia two calamities. In the latter part of the nineteenth century it lost its access to the sea upon defeat by Chile. More serious, early in the 1930's it fought and lost the Chaco War with Paraguay—"two bald men fighting for a comb," as one wit expressed it. Still, this war served to intensify a feeling of nationalism already held by many educated Bolivians who realized their country's backwardness, and from this nationalistic tradition the regime which has been in power since 1952, the National Revolutionary Movement *(MNR)*, has developed and drawn its essential strength.

The decade before the accession to power of the *MNR* regime in 1952 saw a dramatic series of events, including one of the truly shocking incidents in modern Latin American history. In December, 1943, a nationalistic coalition of Chaco War veterans, led by Major Gualberto Villarroel, and civilian *MNR* elements, led by Víctor Paz Estenssoro, seized control of the government, aided by the new "colonels' clique" now in control of Argentina. Because of its pro-Fascist ties, the new government was not recognized by the United States until June, 1944. In July, 1946, a revolution broke out against the repressive regime, sparked by a teachers' strike and involving street fighting in La Paz. The climax of this bloody uprising was reached when the mob hurled President Villarroel to his death from a balcony of the government's palace and strung his body up on a lamppost in the main plaza. Paz escaped into Argentina, where Perón gave him a government position.

Though Paz accused the tin interests of inciting the coup, its real impact on him and the *MNR* leadership was much deeper. Disillusioned by the results of their alliance with the army, they concluded that a policy of "political enlightenment," via agitation, propaganda, and strikes, was needed to win mass support. Five years later this policy paid dividends. Prevented from assuming presidency after winning a clear election plurality (45 per cent), Paz, with the aid of an armed workers' militia, crushed the army and seized the power. In April, 1952, he was accorded a hero's

161

welcome in Bolivia's 179th governmental overturn since its liberation from Spain in 1825. For the first time this was a real revolution, with a broad political and social base.

The MNR today is composed mostly of younger, university-trained men. It has the backing of most urban middle- and lower-income groups, virtually all of the organized labor and the peasants, and a few wealthy people. That is, practically all of the Indians, most of the people of mixed blood, and some of the whites support the regime. The shattered army has now been rebuilt along lines more politically favorable to the MNR. The Church, at first doubtful, has since been reassured that no attacks against it are intended and has extended its benevolent neutrality—which an increase of 50 per cent in the government revenues allocated for Church support has undoubtedly helped make more benevolent.

The members of the opposition, many of whom are in prison or exile, consist primarily of wealthy whites, former army officers, and the owners of the expropriated tin mines. They are represented primarily by the Bolivian Socialist Falange (FSB), which has strongly authoritarian, corporative leanings. The MNR regime, despite Paz's Argentine background, has been free of significant influence from any of the other Latin American countries. Naturally, encouragement of traditional Brazilian-Argentine rivalry can work to Bolivia's advantage.

Politically, the accomplishments of the MNR regime have been impressive. It has established effective control over the entire country. True, there has been unrest in the provinces, owing to seizures of lands by Indians whose hopes have been aroused by the agrarian reform, but it has been less than was anticipated. The labor confederation, especially the tin miners' federation, headed by Juan Lechín, has considerably increased its political power within the regime. Paz, nevertheless, appears definitely to be the dominant leader and, barring a sharp deterioration, to be capable of holding the more radical labor element in line. In 1956 Vice-President Siles Zuazo was elected president to succeed Paz. Through the end of that year he followed the moderate line of Paz, with a somewhat firmer direction of the nation's economy.

Suffrage is now universal. In an attempt to increase literacy (only 20 per cent) so that the mass of the people can become more effective politically and economically, the regime has allocated up to about 50 per cent of the national budget to education, in contrast to the former 5 per cent. Social security has been extended and an effort has been made to give everyone a living wage.

Nationalization of tin has been the most sensational and in many ways the most difficult revolutionary measure undertaken by the new regime. Bolivia is a high-cost producer of tin. The mines are located in almost inaccessible mountains at elevations between 12,000 and 18,000 feet; the labor of extracting is therefore slow, and the cost of shipping the ore to market extremely high. Bolivian tin has sold on world markets largely via the tin cartels, which allocated a much higher quota for the cheaper ores from Malaya. In the last several years American purchases have absorbed the bulk of the tin output. When these purchases ceased for a time during the Korean War, Bolivia was thrown into a turmoil, American relations with the country became strained, and there were even mutterings of invoking the "economic aggression" clause (Article 16) of the Charter of the OAS.

Until 1952 the great majority of the tin production was owned by the "Big Three" companies, Hochschild, Aramyo, and Patiño. American interests were estimated at only about $7 to $8 million (28 per cent), all in the Patiño mines. These three companies had made themselves foreign entities when their capital increased enormously in 1923, and before the government had established taxes on mining utilities and prescribed some social laws. Much of the capital was owned by absentee Bolivians. One of the curiosities of history was Simón Patiño, owner of the Patiño mines and one of the richest men on earth. He spent most of his adult life outside his country, allegedly because, being part Indian, he had once been refused admission to an upper-crust Bolivian country club! The MNR had long contended that the tin interests had "used their power for political domination of the country, paid disproportionately small taxes, drained the country of resources without reinvesting enough of the wealth produced, and exploited

163

Bolivian workers."* These charges, strongly reminiscent of those levied by Lázaro Cárdenas in 1938 against the American and British oil companies in Mexico, were exaggerated, particularly when compared with the record of the last few years before 1952. That there was some truth in them, however, could not be denied.

In recent years tin exports, which have normally accounted for over 70 per cent of Bolivia's foreign-exchange revenues, have fluctuated wildly in price— from a low of $0.74 per pound in 1949, when the United Kingdom flooded the market by selling off its war stocks, to a high of $1.90 in February, 1951, with the Korean War, and back down to $1.03 in July, 1951. The last tumble was caused by the United States' refusal to buy any more tin at the higher price, with the Senate Armed Services Committee charging that the United States was being gouged by the tin interests. In the ensuing bargaining, the Bolivian negotiators held out for a price higher than the Reconstruction Finance Corporation (sole purchaser) was willing to pay. The principal arguments of the Bolivians were highly revealing. They pointed out that Bolivia had supplied the United States when the latter was cut off from Asian supplies during World War II and that the war had led to consumption of most of Bolivia's high-grade ores, with the result that only the lower-grade, high-cost ores remained. In other words, Americans should remember that they had made extensive use of Bolivian tin in time of emergency, that they were thus largely responsible for the present higher price of tin, and that by implication they had an obligation to be liberal toward Bolivia now. The principal Yankee arguments were that the lower price would give Bolivian producers more than a fair profit and that the large increase in production at the beginning of the Korean War was "opportunistic." Evident from this conflict in views was the fact that, while Bolivia was naturally thinking of its own *national* economic interest, the United States was at this time thinking primarily in terms of the big companies. Later it too was to view

*Senate Committee on Banking and Currency, 83rd Congress, *Study of Latin America* (Capehart Report), Report No. 1082 (Washington, D.C.), p. 54.

the question of tin purchases more from the point of view of Bolivian national interest, or, perhaps better, mutual national interests.

Meanwhile tin was piling up on the docks at Antofagasta, Chile, unemployment was spreading rapidly in the mines, and labor unrest and antagonism mounted toward the hated "Ring" (as the "Big Three" were called). This impasse was what the *MNR* regime inherited in 1952; that it was in a dilemma is not surprising. On the one hand, political pressures for nationalization were almost irresistible. On the other, to move hastily without adequately trained government technicians and without due regard to the interests of the owners, might worsen the financial situation by decreasing production and ending all chances of agreement with Washington. Finally in October, 1952, the decision, probably sooner or later inevitable, was for expropriation. The "Big Three" were nationalized, and title was transferred to a new government entity, the "Bolivian Mining Corporation." The companies who had valued their properties at slightly less than $100 million were offered $22 million compensation. Furthermore, they were billed $250 million, more than twenty times the compensation, allegedly for back taxes, duties, and profits on illegal foreign exchange transactions!

Only one other expropriation of foreign interests in Latin American history had caused a greater initially adverse impact—that of the petroleum companies in Mexico. The big difference in the Bolivian case from the American point of view was that primarily non-American interests were involved and were therefore the ones to protest. It is interesting to note that President-elect Siles Zuazo, while a delegate to the United Nations, had introduced the resolution encouraging nationalization of resources which was passed. The signing of the expropriation decree before 30,000 cheering miners symbolized the fulfillment of one of the *MNR's* major pledges but represented the beginning of a long and arduous road.

Next to the tin expropriation, the most immediately revolutionary aspect of the new regime has been the agrarian reform. The parceling out of the large estates (some with 12 million acres), on which the peasants had lived as semislaves, is proceeding at a varying pace in the different provinces. Under the law the beneficiaries receive farms ranging from 25 to 2,000 acres, depending on the quality of the land. The landowners, to their dissatisfaction, receive twenty-five-year government bonds in payment. On one occasion Paz said: " . . . we have created a capitalist revolution with our agrarian reform. It can be compared to what occurred in Europe under feudalism." His minister of rural affairs explained that the government wished to avoid the Mexican mistake, which was to give the peasants communal land but not the title (not an accurate appraisal), and the Guatemalan tactic, which was to make the Communist-dominated government the landlord. In Bolivia the peasant has been declared the owner, except where the Indians have preferred communal holdings. It is obviously far too early to pronounce any satisfactory judgment on the Bolivian agrarian reform, but it appears to be taking place with less turmoil and disorder than either the Mexican reform or the Guatemalan one in its later stages. As was to be expected, it has had an initially adverse economic impact. The farmers, with their newly acquired lands, have not yet increased production of scarce foodstuffs, and in fact have consumed the food themselves, thus making domestic foodstuffs even scarcer in the cities.

Despite clamors of the labor confederation for nationalization of the British-owned railways and other public utilities, Paz promised that there would be no more expropriations, and through 1956 the new Siles regime adhered to this policy. Nor would Paz grant labor's demands for establishment of worker-control units in various industries. On the contrary, Paz stated that Bolivia wanted foreign private investments in oil, manufacturing, food-packing, and other industries ancillary to agriculture. There have been indications that foreign investors, at first naturally hesitant, are becoming interested. The best example is in petroleum, where, as a result of an unusually liberal petroleum code (in stark contrast to those in Argentina and Brazil) an American producer has already brought in a new field in southern Bolivia, and negotiations have

166

been completed by an American concern to construct a pipe line
for transmission of oil to Argentina. Consequently, Bolivia is already
self-sufficient in petroleum and expects soon to export oil in quantity
to all her neighbors. With the $5 million garnered by petroleum
exports to Argentina, she will be able to import vitally needed
wheat. Mineral exports will continue to bulk large in her exports,
perhaps as much as 90 per cent, but petroleum will play a much
larger role and tin a much smaller one than heretofore. Another
important accomplishment has been the completion of the vital
300-mile Santa Cruz-Cochabamba highway, which will at last provide a good connection between the agricultural eastern lowland and
the high *altiplano* region. Wheat and potatoes, increased under
Point Four aid, can now be interchanged among the two regions.

Thus the *MNR* regime has gone a long way towards implementing
its revolutionary policies. Grave problems nevertheless confront it.
Perhaps the greatest single one is a scarcity of personnel. There
are simply not enough civil servants, either senior or junior, with
ability and experience to handle the multifaceted problems. Only
recently has there been established a university program for training in public administration, industrial management, or even technology. Succeeding dictators and their cliques have overstaffed
the government bureaus with incompetent supporters and relatives,
and petty *caudillos* have expanded their power at lower levels.
The salary of the president is only about $3,600, and the range
for lower-ranking officials can well be imagined. In contrast, the
salary of the general manager of a mining corporation is $18,000,
while that for a manager of an average-sized manufacturing concern
is the same as that of the president. Naturally, except at the top
level, most able people have tended to look toward private enterprise
for a career. The pressures to incite governmental corruption are
obviously great.

As a result, the tasks of keeping the tin industry on its feet,
administering the agrarian reform in orderly fashion, and trying
to keep inflation from becoming critically acute strain to the limit
the slender human resources. In the instance of tin, the situation
has been aggravated by factors beyond Bolivia's control. The world

167

price has plummeted to around $0.80 per pound, and production costs have risen with the higher wages that have had to be paid to the miners. Most of the experienced foreign engineers have left the country, though a few have decided to work for the new government. Virtually no profits have been made and most of the smaller mines have had to close. The regime has been fearful of closing any of the larger mines, since this would throw thousands of men out of work and invite political disaster.

One plan has been to move about 10 per cent of the miners to the Santa Cruz farming region, although the terminal payments and bonuses involved have caused a heavy financial drain on the country's meager reserves. The government also hopes to install a smelter, in order to cut marketing costs by exporting pure tin instead of concentrates. In June, 1953, a contract was signed with the Patiño interests to repay them on the basis of tin and tungsten retentions when the price is above $0.80. To the frustration of those interests, it has never gone substantially above this figure, at least through 1956. One sees in the above moves two principal objectives: to nationalize completely the tin industry, and to relieve Bolivia of its excessive dependence on tin.

Owing largely to the ailing condition of the tin industry, but also to the continuing need to import essential foodstuffs and the short-term adverse impact of the agrarian reform on the domestic food supply, the fiscal and financial situations of the government have become critical. The printing press has been used to multiply money in circulation, and Bolivia has suffered the worst inflation in Latin America, worse even than that in Chile or in Brazil. The boliviano has since 1952 depreciated many times in relation to the dollar. Fortunately, the one item that has not gone up greatly in price is essential food, prices of which have been kept down by a system of competitive bids for food imports.

Politically, the chief problem faced by Paz's dominant wing of the MNR and by his successor, Siles, is to keep in line the labor confederation bossed by Lechín, and at the same time to accord labor the political power and economic advantages it rightly deserves. Lechín apparently resigned his position as minister of

168

labor in order to devote full time to retaining control of the labor movement. His "Pulacayo Thesis" in 1946 employed such phrases as: "direct mass action, worker-operated mines, general strike, and the elimination of private property." Since then, labor has been given such excessive legal benefits that their application could not be enforced. In the light of the above "thesis," the great aspirations of labor, and the fact that it still possesses considerable quantities of arms, the possibility that the more radical *MNR* wing might attempt to seize control of Bolivia cannot be discounted. Apparently, however, Lechín became somewhat less radical with age and maturity, and is making an attempt to collaborate with Siles and act as a restraining influence on labor extremists.

One final problem must be considered—the Communists. The Senate Security Subcommittee report cited previously indicates a total strength of around 3,500, by no means a small number for a country with Bolivia's tiny elite of leaders. Fortunately, the Communists have been split for several years into two competing parties. One, a Trotskyite deviationist group, has seemed to be the more powerful, particularly in the labor confederation. The other, Soviet-dominated, appears to be more influential in university circles. Paz admitted that there were still some Communists lodged in lower-level government jobs. He explained, however, that it was not yet feasible to dispense with the services of any of the government's few trained administrators. The important point is that in contrast to what happened in Guatemala, Communists have not been guiding the course of the revolution in Bolivia, and indeed through 1956 did not even exercise a perceptible influence on it. Nevertheless, given a significant economic deterioration in Bolivia, with a probably ensuing split between the moderate Paz-Siles and radical Lechín wings, the Communists could probably begin to play an important role.

With the advent to power of the *MNR* and its nationalization of tin, the United States has been faced with one of its most critical decisions involving Latin America in the contemporary era. It has been confronted with the following charges circulated widely abroad by the tin interests and other opposition elements: the MNR regime is in reality led by dedicated Communists; private property is on the way out; the Church is being persecuted; 6,000 people are in prison; if the United States helps Bolivia now, it is merely helping a Trojan horse which can become the Communist center for South America. The president of the new regime was once labeled as a pro-Nazi, and the United States delayed recognition of a government in which he took part for that reason. Though no proof has been discovered that Lechín, the "number two" man—at least in the Paz regime—is a Communist, he has certainly made many statements in the past which sound like the party line. Furthermore, Bolivia is of no apparent strategic value to the United States from a military point of view, and in view of the ample stock piles of tin, its production of that commodity is not needed in normal times. The only value of the tin is its hemispheric location for emergency use. In view of Bolivia's inaccessibility, traditional political instability, and economic backwardness, some pessimists have argued that it hardly deserves to exist as a separate nation (calling to mind similar shortsighted remarks about Paraguay and Ecuador). They suggest that it might well be divided among its more powerful neighbors, with Argentina and Brazil getting the major portions. These statements are mentioned only to show why we should examine more carefully the reasons for the United States' real interest in what happens in Bolivia.

Fortunately certain American statesmen have adopted an intelligent long-range view of the Bolivian problem. They agree that without substantial and quick economic aid from the United States, the MNR regime would collapse within a few months. That regime, though it contains a few unpalatable elements from the American point of view and can be characterized accurately as leftist, is a genuine nationalist revolutionary regime without any significant Communist influence. It has expropriated the tin mines, in accordance with a long-standing pledge for nationalization, but has made the best settlement it could, in view of its critical financial straits, with the tin interests. Also, its leaders have shown no further tendency to expropriate private foreign investments; indeed, they have seemed anxious to obtain more investments in certain fields.

Even if the government were to expropriate the railroads and utilities, however, there are much deeper considerations to keep in mind. Should the regime collapse, what would be the prospects? They certainly contain little that is pleasant to contemplate. The best guesses are that either the opposition *FSB* would seize power temporarily and be overthrown in a short time, to be followed for a while by the extreme leftist elements in the labor movement and then chaos; or that the order would be labor-*FSB*-chaos. The final outcome appears the same, no matter how the changes are rung, and it is not hard to see that the Communists would stand to gain immeasurably from this concatenation of calamities.

Edward J. Sparks, the capable American ambassador to Bolivia through 1955, was from the first alive to the realities of the country, while Dr. Milton Eisenhower, visiting Bolivia in July, 1953, alerted top-level officials in Washington that substantial economic aid from the United States was needed urgently. Such aid obviously would also have its crucial political and psychological implications for the stability of the government, for it would clearly indicate that the United States approved of the new regime and was giving it moral as well as material support.

An initial grant of $9 million was made, subsequently expanded to $14 million, in the form of emergency foodstuffs, agricultural products, insecticides, machinery, tools, and broadened Point Four technical assistance. The last-named has been concentrated in the fields of education, agriculture, public health, and civil aviation, all obviously essential to Bolivia's development. In addition, the Santa Cruz-Cochabamba highway had been built largely by means of an Export-Import Bank (American government) loan. The *MNR* regime requested aid amounting to $50-60 million in foodstuffs, grants, and loans through 1958 or 1959 which appeared almost certain to be granted. At the end of this time it has estimated that its economy should be viable, unless the tin market goes to pieces. The United States was at first reluctant to purchase any sizable amount of tin and thus seem to encourage expropriation, with only vague promises of compensation. When the situation deteriorated, however, it signed a one-year contract to purchase about 15,000 tons of tin concentrates at the going world price. There were indications that this might be done in the future on a year-to-year basis. At any rate it is clear that continued American aid is necessary to keep the regime in power.

Economic aid has thus far been the most critical need. But here is a clear case where political and ideological support also are important in themselves. Visits to the United States by Bolivian labor and intellectual leaders could be vital in orienting the new regime and in maintaining the country's present strong pro-American outlook. In particular, serious consideration should be given to inviting Juan Lechín to the United States, notwithstanding his radical background. Contacts with the AFL-CIO labor federation and a general view of the great country which he has never seen could help swing him more to the American side. It is probably safe to guess that the Soviet-Chinese blocs have already extended to him an invitation to visit the "peoples'" labor organizations behind the Iron Curtain. He might well accept this invitation out of sheer curiosity, but for the obviously well-founded fear that it would alienate the United States.

Bolivia has been rescued from chaos. What is the underlying significance of the courageous decision on the Bolivian problem for American foreign policy toward Latin America? It has conclusively shown that situations may arise in areas of Latin America where American strategic interests are not directly threatened, and yet where the United States cannot remain aloof. Nor can the great northern republic view with unconcern the probability that without American aid any Latin American country, however remote, may sooner or later either have a Communist or other anti-American regime, or become a chaotic power vacuum. Aside from the principle involved, such a country might well become a focus of infection for other nations in South America. As we have seen, this the United States was to learn in Guatemala, where a situation at one point roughly analogous to the Bolivian had been allowed

172

to deteriorate to a stage at which unpalatably drastic measures finally became necessary.

But this is purely a negative point of view; there is also a strong affirmative side to American aid. At last the United States has shown itself actively on the side of the revolution that is sweeping certain parts of Latin America and will undoubtedly soon permeate others. In many regions of the world, the Soviet Union and the Chinese Communists have seemed to be in favor of progressive radicalism. In Bolivia the United States has shown that when revolutionary change is a genuine national aspiration, it will gamble on it. Meanwhile, the rest of Latin America has been watching closely the Bolivian policy of the United States and for the most part approves its truly farsighted decision. Of course, one must remember that the political situation can change suddenly in Bolivia, and that the commitment and period of "watchful waiting" are by no means completed. But the prospects seem promising; more so, frankly, than they do in Guatemala. Even if the *MNR* regime does collapse, it is our view that the United States was right in backing it. And this success has been achieved without "intervening" in internal Bolivian affairs, according to our definition of the term. Strong American action was undeniably brought to bear to help guide the course of events. Yet to characterize the Bolivian case as "Yankee intervention" is to misuse this term in such a way as to inhibit gravely the proper application of American influence in Latin America.

-XI-

Argentina: Despite Perón

Far removed from the United States are the two major powers of Latin America, Argentina and Brazil. At inter-American conferences these two nations, with Mexico, have generally played the most important roles. The United States has had contrasting experiences with the two South American giants, but except for one unfortunate affair, Yankee intervention has not taken place as it has in the Caribbean area. Yet Yankee "influence" or "support" has been employed on several occasions, particularly in Brazil.

Argentina is the eighth largest country in area in the world and the second largest in Latin America. Its predominantly white population of about 19 million has the highest literacy in all Latin America (around 90 per cent). Argentina's population is concentrated heavily around one great metropolis, Buenos Aires, the largest and most highly developed city of Latin America and one of the world's great urban centers. The bulk of the population is well fed, the climate temperate. These characteristics, combined with extensive European immigration and one of the most fertile farming areas in the world, the *pampa*, have made Argentina one of the few Latin American nations not to be classified by most economists as "underdeveloped." Through its huge exports of meat and wheat, Argentina has become one of the world's great trading nations. Though it is deficient in most mineral resources, it produces about 40 per cent of its petroleum requirements. Argentina's wealth and prosperity have long contributed to a feeling of pride and superiority over other Latin American peoples. With the exception of its small, culturally similar, next-door neighbor, Uruguay, Argentina is the only nation in Latin America which has steadily maintained a primarily European orientation.

Our focus in this chapter must necessarily be to a great extent

174

on American relationships with the Perón regime, but as the chapter title implies, we shall consider these relations from a longer-range point of view. First, we should like to take a broad look at the Perón regime, especially its foreign relations, and then speculate as to the probable course which the Argentine may follow in the near future. From one perspective, Perón might be regarded as having recognized and then accelerated with forceful means a revolutionary change in the social and political structure of Argentina. Until 1916 a relatively few great cattle and wheat barons made up the landed oligarchy ruling the country. From 1916 to 1930 the middle-class Radical Party held the reins. The period 1930 to 1943 was largely reactionary; a dominant coalition of conservatives and military leaders resented the middle-class domination and feared the growing restlessness of labor. Perón himself perceived that it was impolitic to block indefinitely social and economic progress for the working man. With the essential aid of the army he captured the labor movement, gave it most of the advantages it sought, and together with his wife, Evita, made it the principal pillar of his popular support.

Perón's second major appeal, which cut across many classes, was to the nationalistic sentiment of Argentines. By expropriating the large British and American concerns, he achieved the "economic independence" of Argentina, and by exalting Argentine nationality and superiority he catered to the feeling of national pride.

Perón ruled dictatorially by a combination of the "carrot and the stick." The stick was frequently employed in the early years of his regime; later the carrot was more in evidence, as he became more confident of his stability and the opposition grew progressively more divided. His feud with the Church, however, reflected his uneasiness over the continued existence of a traditional institution which still exercised influence among many people, also over the increasing civilian opposition organizing around the Christian Democratic Party. It is also now clear in retrospect that dissidence increased sharply among the officers' ranks of the armed forces. Finally, toward the end of his regime, the previous fanatical support of organized labor for Perón unquestionably diminished. This was partly because Perón at last decided that favoring labor at the expense of the employers and middle class had reached a point of diminishing returns. Nevertheless labor, now 70 per cent organized as against less than 10 per cent before Perón, was still better off than it had been, and even after the fall of Perón large segments continued loyal to *peronista* institutions, because of the benefits, both material and psychological, which his regime undeniably gave them. The gains were material largely in terms of fringe benefits, such as holidays, bonuses, and pensions, rather than in real wages; and psychological in terms of the supposed elevation of labor to a place of greater dignity in the national life. Though the legal Communist Party (about 35,000) may have achieved long-range gains from the dictatorship, it does not appear in the last few years to have been a major political factor—not so much as the one in Brazil, for example.

Perón was finally overturned by a military coup in September, 1955. Let us remember, however, that this amazing ruler was able to maintain himself in power for about a decade, in the face of constant domestic and foreign opposition and predictions that he was "about to go." His staying power was due largely to his shrewd ability to "sway with the tide." Hence one can say that, aided by the departure of fanatical Evita, he allowed a Thermidorian reaction to set in after the Jacobin extremes. Sensing the need for greater attention to the middle-income groups, and wishing to create a political counterweight to the labor confederation, he gave his blessing to the establishment of a General Economic Confederation, composed of middle-income workers and the professional classes. Furthermore, Perón encouraged the entrance of private capital, both domestic and foreign, into many sectors of the economy theretofore reserved exclusively for governmental control, although this brought him into conflict with those more extreme elements of his party who had been nurtured for years on his ultranationalistic line. The sudden switch proved too abrupt for them. Thus "justicialism," formerly the middle way between collectivism (that is, Communism) and capitalism, seemed to be

176

veering more toward the latter. Further substantial industrialization, however, depended (and still does) largely on foreign capital and credits. Toward the end of Perón's regime, general economic conditions deteriorated, owing to failure to maintain a high level of exports with which in turn to acquire essential imports, to poorly managed, inflationary fiscal and financial policies, and to a rampant corruption in the government.

It is only accurate to point out that the fall of Perón was not caused to any large degree by poor economic conditions evident at that time or by a mass uprising. It was simply a military overturn. No doubt this reflected the wishes of increasingly large numbers of the people, especially those in the upper-middle-income brackets. But a good many of the lower-income population were anxious to conserve the gains made under Perón and were uneasy about their lot under any new regime.

Through 1956 a military junta, balanced uneasily between army and navy, ruled Argentina, with elections called for late 1957. Dissident army groups remained a threat to the junta, which was confronted with probably the most severe problems ever faced by an Argentine government. A decade of *peronismo* had left the country fragmented and financially almost prostrate, particularly in terms of foreign-exchange needs. The governmental bureaucracy had hypertrophied to the point where its payroll expenses had become enormous. The transportation and power systems were in near crisis, and development of petroleum resources was needed to relieve the country of the heavy drain full imports were putting on its foreign exchange. But nationalistic sentiment, as in Brazil, prevented the use of substantial foreign capital and knowhow for this job. Meat and wheat exports, Argentina's staples of life, had seriously diminished. For the first time in many years, Argentine economic missions were abroad seeking loans in both the United States and Europe to shore up the economy.

In short, the years of corruption and mismanagement of resources by Perón and his cohorts, especially toward the end of the regime, had left the country in a parlous economic state indeed. Politically, tensions would have to subside before the country would be ready

177

once again to have a democratic regime. One trouble was that the strongest candidate to appear on the horizon through 1956, Arturo Frondizi, the Radical Party head, was reportedly bitterly opposed by the armed forces.

As the year 1956 began, Argentina's political future, on which so much else depended, appeared to rest on the answers to three major questions: (1) Would the armed forces desist from personal political ambition and turn control over to responsible civilian elements? (2) If they did not, would the majority of the Argentine people, mindful of earlier democratic traditions and disgusted with the later years of the Perón regime especially, force them to throw the country open to democratic elections? (3) Would whatever elements gained eventual control of Argentine destinies understand that a change had occurred in the political and social structure of Argentina in the last decade, especially with reference to the position of organized labor?

Particularly because of the *volte-face* which Perón made toward the end in his policy toward the United States, it seems wise to take a brief look at past trends in the southern nation's foreign policy. Until about 1900, Argentina was not really significant in inter-American relations. From that year until 1953, it challenged American leadership at the various conferences and attempted to set itself up as a leader of the Latin American nations. This behavior, for which there are several explanations, was primarily caused by Argentina's increasing urge to counter Yankee influence in South America. Before World War II, Argentina felt no need to align itself with any other Latin American country, or with the United States. It was able to maintain this splendid isolation in the Western Hemisphere by remaining economically dependent upon Great Britain, the leading world power. The fact that the United States would not buy an important Argentine export product, fresh beef (allegedly because of the hoof-and-mouth disease), further hampered relations between the two rivals.

World War II upset the balance of international power and isolated Argentina completely. Great Britain emerged greatly

178

weakened, and the United States and the Soviet Union became the two power leaders. During the war, Argentina, though officially neutral, had turned to Germany as the probable emerging world power and best counterweight to American hegemony in the Western Hemisphere. After Germany's fall, Argentina sought to get back into the good graces of the inter-American community. Soon afterward, however, it established diplomatic relations with the Soviet-bloc countries, probably with the idea of having as a potential ally the other leading world power—a rival of the United States. Perón, however, never committed Argentina to the Soviet Union. Such an opportunistic commitment would have been too much even for him to explain to the *argentinos*. On the other hand, until 1953, neither did he commit Argentina to *rapprochement* with the United States. Instead he held to a proud and completely independent "third position," which in practice was more anti-American than anti-Soviet, because the United States obviously has more direct involvement with Argentina than has the Soviet Union.

Meanwhile, postwar American policy toward Argentina changed abruptly from one of strong opposition to the Perón regime to one varying between friendly diplomatic correctness and extreme cordiality. The opposition of Cordell Hull and the speeches of Ambassador Spruille Braden in effect attacking Perón, and the publication of the "Blue Book" exposing Nazi intrigue in Argentina, all had the effect, opposite to that intended, of assuring Perón's election in 1946 and strengthening Argentine ultranationalists. Here was an obvious case of Yankee diplomatic intervention, one that backfired. Since then, with Fascism no longer acute and Communism the principal menace, American policy toward Argentina has had two principal objectives: 1) to prevail upon Argentina to cooperate in the strengthening of hemispheric military defenses against Communism, and (2) to promote American economic interests in Argentina. A goodly succession of businessmen ambassadors who were extremely friendly on a personal basis with Perón were sent to Buenos Aires. The last ambassador under the Perón regime, the late Albert Nufer, was a career diplomat with a good understanding of Argentine economics and was kept at his post for several years. A third objective was contemplated by some who viewed Perón as an effective force against Communism. Allegedly Perón could be of considerable assistance in putting down Communist movements in neighboring countries. Also, *peronista* political influence would supposedly be an effective anti-Communist "ism" appealing to influential elements in other Latin American countries. This idea did not gain many adherents, for it was outweighed by logical fears that the expansion of *peronista* influence would in its turn contribute to anti-Yankeeism. It was sheer anathema to most of the American press, and to American labor leaders and liberals, who opposed Perón strongly as being a totalitarian dictator.

Particularly after Perón's seizure of the famous Buenos Aires newspaper, *La Prensa,* American newspapers and periodicals were unanimously opposed to him. No other regime outside the Iron Curtain encountered such a solid front of hostility from the American press. Well might Perón rue the day he closed down *La Prensa!*

During these postwar years, Perón sought to obtain a more important role for Argentina in international organizations. In the Organization of American States his general technique was to resist effective regional organization, to accept it nominally if overruled, but to fail to ratify agreements. Thus at the inter-American defense meeting in Rio in 1947, Argentina espoused the general Latin American cause against the United States when the former argued in vain for a Marshall Plan for Latin America. It also demanded unanimity on voting in the new defense organization, which would thus allow for a veto power. Defeated on this, it bowed to the majority will but failed to ratify the Rio treaty. At Bogotá in 1948, Perón spoke out in favor of bilateral rather than multilateral agreements. The Argentine delegates refused to accept "union" or "association" as descriptive of the new inter-American community, allegedly because it connoted a superstate. They finally agreed to "organization." The delegates were defeated in their opposition to granting political powers to the council of the OAS but were successful in opposing the creation of a permanent military agency. Perón made a revealing commentary on his feelings about the new organization when he stated that "the best way to consolidate Pan-Americanism" was to put an end to "spoliation" of Latin America by capitalist imperialism. When the Korean War broke out in 1950, Argentina at last ratified the Rio treaty and as a reward received a credit from the Export-Import Bank of $125 million to liquidate the overdue balances of American exporters. Argentine public opinion would not allow Perón to lend any fighting assistance, however, and he extended no other aid of any real significance.

During the first few postwar years Argentina was not happy with its role in the United Nations, nor with that of the United States. In the League of Nations, the United States had not played any part; in the United Nations it had a major one. But during the Berlin Blockade in 1948, Argentina secured some measure of limelight in attempting to bring about a solution of the impasse. One reason why some of the other nations in the United Nations were not kindly disposed toward Argentina was that it had allegedly taken advantage of international postwar distress by wheat-profiteering and at the same time refusing to extend relief and rehabilitation to refugees. Sensitive to these charges, Argentina replied that it had made gifts of $94 million in beef and wheat and had extended $151 million in credits and long-term government loans.

Meanwhile Perón sought to extend *peronista* influence throughout Latin America by means of bilateral economic agreements, labor attachés, and finally, in 1952, by the establishment of *Agrupación de Trabajadores Latinoamericanos Sindicalistas (ATLAS)*, a *peronista* labor confederation for Latin America, which would rival the Communist confederation *Confederación de Trabajadores de América Latina (CTAL)*, and the non-Communist *Organización Regional Interamericana de Trabajadores (ORIT)*. Economic agreements, primarily to expand trade, were completed with Chile, Bolivia, Ecuador, and Colombia. The most significant one involved exchanges of Argentine meat and wheat for Chilean coal, iron ore, steel, and other industrial materials. Except in Paraguay, Argentine political influence did not attain significant proportions

181

in these countries. The attachés gained some influence among labor groups in Peru and Cuba, and a few labor leaders were invited to the Peronista Trade Union School in Buenos Aires. Neither this phase nor the later activities of *ATLAS* appeared to have much real success. Probably of greater influence than either the trade or labor tactics were the Argentine sojourns of certain military officers who were later to become the dictators of their countries, among them Manuel Odría of Peru and Pérez Jiménez of Venezuela. These Latin American leaders had no intention of allowing Perón, or Argentina, to gain any important direct influence in their countries, but they did have occasion to study firsthand *peronista* organizational, labor, and propaganda tactics.

In retrospect it now appears that, beginning around 1951, Perón decided to seek a *rapprochement* with the United States. This radical change in his foreign-policy orientation was based primarily on economic considerations. Perón was having difficulty in achieving the industrial objectives of his First Five-Year Plan and felt strongly the need for foreign capital and technical assistance, available mostly in the United States. After the bonanza years following World War II, Argentina encountered much greater difficulty in disposing of its exports, particularly its wheat. Furthermore, an almost unbroken drought from 1949 to 1952 caused a considerable decline in agricultural output of all kinds.

Perón, however, was in a delicate position insofar as openly seeking foreign aid was concerned. Argentina, not regarding itself as an underdeveloped country, had never accepted any Point Four technical assistance, and Perón had vowed that he would never accept a foreign loan. Private foreign capital investment and better credit terms for Argentine importers seemed to be the solutions. There were also important political deterrents to his seeking an accommodation. Eva Perón was one of the most extreme Yankeephobes, and important elements in both the *peronista* party and the opposition Radicals were extremely nationalistic. They espoused nationalization vociferously and were against investments by big American business concerns in Argentina.

Evita's death removed one obstacle; the objections of the oppo-

182

sition and Perón's own party were overridden with great difficulty. More difficulty was encountered with Perón's own supporters, but the dictator temporarily conquered their objections. The change of administration in the United States, and the accession of a fellow general to power also eased the matter. In March, 1953, it was announced that a law was being prepared to attract foreign capital. But before the "carrot" was actually made available, the "stick" was applied once again. The officially controlled press denounced the Yankees as "imperialist enemies," and American press and news services were boycotted. Milton Eisenhower's visit in July, 1953, paved the way for settlement of the problems and for the readmission of a number of American periodicals to Argentina. Moreover, Perón undertook some drastic measures against Communist activities, but pointed out that there was "no price tag on his friendship."

Perón was not very successful in attracting private American investment. His petroleum negotiations with the Standard Oil Company of California were later repudiated by the succeeding regime, in full accord with the nationalistic public opinion. Henry Kaiser commenced production of Kaiser-Frazer automobiles in return for an assured minimum market, and W. R. Grace and Co. invested in some chemical plants. The Kaiser deal and others made during the Perón regime were for a time held in ill repute but later were approved. American business investors as a whole, however, did not indicate a willingness to invest any new capital in Argentina. While the new law appeared relatively reasonable, no profits had been remitted from Argentina since 1947 on old investments, with the single exception of the remittances made possible in 1950 by the $125 million Export-Import Bank credit. Private investors are naturally more interested in performance than mere legislative enactment. Meanwhile the Export-Import Bank in early 1955 extended another credit to Argentina, this time $60 million to aid in building a large steel mill. One can well imagine that Chile, which had been supplying Argentina with some steel in return for vitally needed foodstuffs, was not happy about this new development. Nor were Argentine exiles, Latin American liberals, and American anti-*peronistas*, who cried loudly that this was another example of our "propping up" dictatorships in this hemisphere.

While his principal needs were economic, Perón was also anxious for military assistance. The Argentine army was apparently not so well equipped as the Brazilian, because most of the sizable amount of funds expended on it were to improve living conditions and transport. Though ostensibly Perón had the army securely under his control, he wanted to gain its active support by improving its matériel situation. A military pact was concluded with the United States in 1954, and the general greatly impressed visiting American military dignitaries with the efficiency of his military machine. This was partly attributable to the attractive dynamism of his personality and the "red carpet" treatment which he extended to influential foreign visitors. Brazil, notwithstanding its unquestioned sincere good will, has not always been able to make an equally favorable impression on American military officials.

Just for good measure, Perón continued to "play both sides of the street." In August, 1953, he concluded a two-way trade agreement totaling $180 million with the Soviet Union, involving an exchange of Soviet coal, oil, lubricants, tractors, oil-drilling equipment, and other machinery for Argentine wool, hides, linseed oil, and tanning extract. The latter items, all nonstrategic, were cleared in advance with the United States, and the agreement did not presage any political commitment. Through 1956, so far as can be determined, the Soviet side of the agreement had been fulfilled to 25 per cent, which was frankly more than most observers had expected. In addition, Argentina has bought on long-term credit large quantities of goods from West Germany, which has utilized some of these credits to invest in Argentine industries. Thus other powers than the United States are strongly interested in the Argentine trade and investment market.

Let us evaluate American policy toward the now fallen Perón dictatorship. Was that policy a wise one? First, foreign-policy officials had to assess whether Perón's broad foreign-policy objective —to make Argentina powerful—was hostile to the security interests of the United States. The answer was probably no, however distasteful this objective might be to certain groups. Then what specifically did Perón want for Argentina? He probably wanted eventually to make Argentina the unquestioned military, political, and economic leader of Latin America, and particularly to carve out a strong sphere of Argentine influence in southern South America. Then, largely as a result of attainment of these objectives, he hoped to establish Argentina as a kind of spokesman in international organizations for Latin America, thereby making it one of the world's influential powers. The supplement of the British publication, *The Economist*, once referred to the "long arm" of Perón reaching up over South America and spoke of "Quislings" in Chile and Argentina's projected *Anschluss* into that country. This undoubtedly is an exaggeration. Apart from other considerations, Perón probably realized that he was simply not strong enough to dominate all of South America, much less Latin America, nor was there much likelihood that he would undertake military aggression against any other country. Nor, despite occasional blustering and sword-rattling, did Argentine nationalists probably think any more (if they ever seriously did) of re-creating the old colonial Viceroyalty of the Rio de la Plata, which would mean completely incorporating the neighboring countries into the Argentine political and economic orbit. As already pointed out, Perón needed from the United States military and economic aid to achieve his objectives. In return he offered his regime as a strong anti-Communist bastion in South America, and he might well have made commitments to aid in the military defense of eastern South America when needed.

Was the United States right in helping strengthen Argentina even if this indirectly aided Perón to entrench himself in power? If one adopts only hemispheric defense and anti-Communism as criteria, the answer seems to be yes, although there were many who questioned the sincerity of Perón's anti-Communism. Argentina is not so strategically important to the United States as, say, Spain, yet it can be one of the principal bulwarks of inter-American defense. If the United States had refused to extend economic aid

185

to Perón, he would have attempted to get it from Soviet, German, and other European sources and would in this case probably have reverted to an anti-Yankee position.

Many people were repelled at the thought of extending any kind of aid to the leading Latin American dictatorship, with its repression of human and civil rights and other Fascist characteristics. Yet the Braden episode showed that application of Woodrow Wilson's "moral imperialism" was counterproductive. There was not much the United States could or should have done to oust the Perón regime. Along with some economic aid and encouragement of private investment in Argentina, our government officials did discreetly urge Perón to ease up on press censorship and on repression of rights and liberties. Perón himself turned out to be sensitive to constant criticism in the foreign press, and this fact proved useful in negotiating with him. One should not have expected too much from a policy of this sort, but the alternative method of semi-quarantine or merely cold indifference had proved fruitless.

To be sure, anti-Perón feeling has continued in the United States to the present day. With the exception of the Guatemalan crisis, no Latin American issue in the last decade has drawn as much attention or provoked as much controversy as American policy toward *peronist* Argentina. The issue even entered the 1956 presidential campaign, a rare occurrence in American political history, when Adlai Stevenson, the Democratic candidate, charged that the Eisenhower Administration not only lent money to Perón which he had used for his own purposes, but had also displayed excessive personal friendliness toward him. Sentiment in the United States tended to favor this interpretation of the State Department's Argentine policy.

But now that the emotions of the moment have subsided it is possible to examine the whole question more objectively. There is no intention of approving the repressive or aggressive features of a now thoroughly discredited dictatorship. Let us remember that we are searching for a policy toward Argentina consistent with the long-term national interests of the United States. Strongly objectionable features of a particular regime or personality may occasionally tempt one to a short-term view, but the long-run perspective must be paramount. The ultimate consideration of the United States government, then, must be the mutual interests of the American and Argentine peoples. A steel mill will in the long run benefit the Argentines. The anti-*peronistas*, both in this country and in Latin America, had a strong case when they said that the United States should not willfully help a repressive dictatorship entrench itself in power, but their case seemed much weaker when they argued that the opposition to Perón was becoming increasingly "alienated" by the friendly relations of the United States with the Perón regime. The fact is that most of the opposition, being strongly nationalistic Argentines, have always been and will continue to be, anti-Yankee in their official orientation. One could sympathize with those who had suffered, but one had to keep in mind that their main objective was to topple Perón, with American aid if possible. The same kind of objective is true of exiles from other Latin American dictatorships. It is not they who exercise responsibility for the conduct of American foreign policy. Had the United States thrown its weight behind the anti-*peronistas*—in other words intervened in Argentina—it would probably in the end have alienated much of Latin America, even including those Argentines and other Latin Americans who professed their distaste for the Perón regime. Surely Americans have not forgotten already the Mexican and Braden episodes and the uncomfortably close call with Guatemala.

Perhaps our foreign-policy makers have something to learn also, in this admittedly difficult test, from the skilled diplomacy of an old and experienced world power like Great Britain. Even though individual Americans may have pinpricks of conscience, their government must steer a cautious course on Argentine policy, without either swinging violently against any regime, or on the other hand, exhibiting a strong personal friendship with its leaders. Both of these courses would almost inevitably cause the United States embarrassment.

Through 1956 official relations between the United States and Argentina continued to be friendly, with the significant difference

187

that now the United States government, press, and public would not have pangs of conscience over such relations with a quasi-Fascist dictator. On its part, Argentina badly needed economic aid from the United States and was now not too proud to ask for loans. For its part, the United States evidenced genuine concern for Argentina's difficult situation and a desire to help. Private investors in general, however, seemed to take the attitude that until Argentina received some major financial transfusions, it was no place to invest one's capital; they would rather wait and see. Through 1956 these financial infiltrations took place slowly; several European countries had worked out with Argentina a system of multilateral payments. Finally, the Argentine economic mission in the United States was successful in obtaining a loan of $100 million from the Export-Import Bank to rehabilitate its transportation system and for industrial and agricultural machinery. Much more than this would be needed, however.

So it would seem that with Perón removed from the scene, and with the new government in dire economic straits and disposed to be genuinely friendly toward the United States, this country would have a rare opportunity to bring about an era of harmonious relations with the southern republic. Such harmony had not really existed since the turn of the century. Now large-scale economic aid could be extended, private investors encouraged to reconsider Argentina as a fruitful area, and ideological relations strengthened, including the exchange-of-persons program. Certainly strategic and political factors, as in Brazil, can be considered as well as purely business ones. There seems to be no further reason for the two dynamic anti-Communist nations to feud with one another, to the advantage of neither and to the detriment of the inter-American community.

We now turn to our last "country case study," that of Brazil. This case illustrates a set of problems at first glance not nearly so dramatic as in the other three, yet the issues at stake are as crucial as those anywhere else in the Western Hemisphere.

188

-XII-

Brazil: A Bulwark Taken for Granted

One speaks of Brazil in superlatives. It is the largest republic and fourth largest country in the world, in area equal to the United States plus a second Texas, and three times as large as Argentina. Its racially tolerant, but only about half-literate population of around 60 million (1956) is over twice that of Mexico and three times that of Argentina. One of its cities, São Paulo, is the largest industrial city of Latin America and the fastest-growing major metropolis in the world. Within Brazil's boundaries are the largest river in the world in terms of volume of water, the Amazon, the largest deposits of pure iron ore, and the largest stands of tropical hardwoods. Through its "cosmic" racial evolution it has developed a most unusual tolerance.

Yet these very superlatives are a disadvantage to Brazil. Brazilians have been so impressed with their unusual geographical phenomena that they have tended to have an apocalyptic vision of the "land of the future," and have therefore not made sufficiently realistic, energetic attempts to develop the country. This self-satisfaction and a certain indolence, bred by the easy existence in the tropical and semitropical climate, have been among the principal factors responsible for Brazil's ranking, thus far, behind Argentina in terms of over-all material progress and standard of living. The fact that the lush tropical capital, Rio de Janeiro, is primarily a playground has been still another deterrent. Two or three southern states of the country, especially progressive São Paulo, have advanced economically much more than most of the rest of Brazil, thus remaining out of balance with their own huge country in general. It is only in this southern area, too, that Brazil thus far really rivals Argentina in general progress.

In sum, what might be called "effective" Brazil is much smaller than the boundaries on the map would indicate, much nearer in size to "effective" Argentina. Its population seen in terms of health, literacy, and productivity is much closer to Argentina's than the respective physical totals would indicate. Nevertheless, its population and its economy are now expanding more rapidly than Argentina's and its standards of living are improving. Certainly its long-range potentialities are substantially greater than those of Argentina. Soon it should be the number one power of Latin America, and Perón and the subsequent Argentine leaders have undoubtedly been aware of this.

The history of Brazil, in contrast to that of Spanish America, has been marked by comparatively little violence. The achievement of independence, the fall of the Empire in 1889, the revolution of 1930 which catapulted Getúlio Vargas into power, his deposition by the army in 1945, and the succession of Vice-President João Café Filho to the presidency after Vargas' suicide—all these transitions took place with little or no bloodshed. True, the revolt of São Paulo against the federal government in 1932, and certain other incidents in the Republican era, have involved some fighting and loss of lives. However, when one considers the history of Mexico, or even of Argentina, Brazil's seems relatively peaceful by comparison. Though there are far more underprivileged people in Brazil than in Argentina, they have never been organized by a demagogic leader of the stamp of Perón or Evita. This has led many observers to say that the tolerant Brazilians are apathetic toward developments and conditions that would arouse the ire of most of the Spanish-American populations. These attitudes now appear to be changing; witness the recent riots over food prices and scarcities and the inadequate urban transportation systems. The partially successful effort led by a labor minister, João Goulart, toward the end of the second Vargas regime, to start a *peronista* type of movement among organized labor may presage the beginning of effective organization of the urban masses. Also, the riots following the suicide of President Vargas indicate that tensions have built up, although the violent outbursts die down quickly.

In large part this comparative lack of violent controversy stems from a strong tradition of paternalism inherent in the Brazilian social structure and entrenched particularly during the half-century (1840-1889) of empire under Dom Pedro II. Dom Pedro ruled his highly centralized government in a firm but benevolent and enlightened fashion. By making use of the supreme "moderative" power bestowed upon him by the constitution, he exercised what has been termed as "constitutional dictatorship" over the country. This paternalistic rule was good for Brazil in that it provided the vast, sprawling country with an efficient administration and prevented the centripetal forces exerted by the provinces from fragmenting Brazil's territory; but on the other hand, it tended to make the Brazilian people increasingly dependent upon guidance from one person instead of able to work out painfully on their own the difficult problems of governing a nation. When the emperor was removed from the scene, Brazil drifted into a kind of regionalism dominated by oligarchical clans, with powerful São Paulo and one or two other southern states monopolizing the leadership of the new republic.

In 1930 another paternalistic ruler, Getúlio Vargas, wrested control of the government away from the dominant groups and for most of the rest of his life was the paramount figure on the Brazilian political scene. He ruled as a complete dictator from 1937 to 1945, and from 1950 until his suicide in 1954 as a constitutionally elected president. His influence over the Brazilian people, however, was eminently paternalistic and is symbolized by the endearing phrase by which he was called, "Father of the Poor." The fact that his dictatorship was largely personal, without even the device of a single-party system, and that he made little use of demagoguery, is further illustration of the sense of personal or familial relationship which permeates the Brazilian ethos. With Vargas gone, the real political question in Brazil may well be: will the people turn to still another "father of the poor?" Or will the country capitalize on the recent broadening of its political base and on its short experience with self-government since Vargas' dictatorship, to develop responsible political parties? Parties would have to face up more urgently than heretofore to Brazil's increas-

191

ingly formidable economic and social problems. Fortunately, the Brazilian army is not so inclined to military rule as the Argentine and acts as a moderate-conservative stabilizing influence, enforcing constitutional processes. It may, however, remove a regime which it feels is not acting in Brazil's best interests.

The four candidates for the presidency in 1955 reflected the diverging currents of opinion concerning the paths toward solution of Brazil's economic and social problems, though they also reflected the usual personalism and selfish interest cliques traditional in Latin American politics. Juscelino Kubitschek, former governor of Minas Gerais, won the election, but did not receive an absolute majority of the votes. He was the candidate of the Social Democratic Party, which had supported Vargas. The illegal Communist Party also swung a lot of votes in his favor, though he emphatically repudiated any ties with the Communists. João Goulart, candidate of Vargas' leftist Labor Party, was elected vice-president. Goulart, who had been Labor Minister under Vargas, was feared by many Brazilians and Americans as pro-Communist, but his later pronouncements and actions, including his friendly visit to the United States, seemed to give assurance that he was not.

It was premature to make any valid predictions about Brazilian political life on the basis of its experience through 1956. True, the responsible ranks of the army had seen to it that the constitutional succession of Kubitschek to the presidency and of Goulart to the vice-presidency took place, even in the face of strong hostility to Goulart from certain significant army groups. And the margin of the electoral victory was slim. It is also true that Kubitschek appeared to be a dynamic individual with a great desire to achieve an ambitious economic program, rather than to spend most of his time "mending political fences." Yet fences must constantly be repaired in Brazil, as in most Latin American countries. There was a real question as to whether the new president could make significant headway against the time-honored Brazilian tradition of political favoritism and benevolent "bossism." Public apathy toward the really constructive measures also was a problem, involving probable mutual sacrifices that would require major support. Only time would tell.

192

Brazil's economic problems have become acute basically because the population is growing at an amazing rate, especially in the large cities; at the same time the country is industrializing rapidly. Acute shortages of power and an inadequate surface transportation system affect the country. As it industrializes and the levels of living go up, demands for imports of both capital goods and consumers' items have increased accordingly. Foreign exchange is needed in an amount far beyond that garnered by exports, of which by far the most important is still coffee. Meanwhile the increasingly large organized urban labor groups are beginning to exert strong political pressure for higher wages and social benefits. Furthermore, the agricultural sector of the economy—still the basic one in terms of the number of people employed—has been sadly neglected, rural labor is in a generally retarded condition, and productivity is low. Hence, there is a scarcity of foodstuffs, which with the poor transportation has caused a sharp increase in the price of foodstuffs in the cities. These cities are experiencing one of the worst inflations in Latin America.

The results of the inability to plan development well are seen from the following examples of economic maladjustments through 1955: grave shortages of power; an extremely inadequate transportation system, especially the railroad; spoilage of more than 25 per cent of Brazil's foodstuffs through lack of storage facilities; grave shortages of well-trained engineers and managers; immobility of urban labor through inflexible labor laws favoring seniority; a tendency to engage in short-term speculative investment rather than long-range productive enterprises (60 per cent of all private Brazilian investment is in Rio and São Paulo, most of it in high-priced residential buildings). As to foreign trade and balance of payments, Brazil had a staggering debt burden of $1.7 billion, with $900 million owed to the United States, a huge petroleum import bill (of Brazil's imports of $1.4 billion in 1955, half went for petroleum, debt services, ocean freight, and wheat, leaving only $700 million for machinery, raw materials, and all other imports); an over-valued currency (official rate 18.78 cruzeiros to $1.00, real value between 60 and 80), which made exports relatively unprofitable. One of the worst problems was the spiraling inflation. From 1939 to 1952 the price inflation in Brazil was 400 per cent; the cost-of-living increase was 455 per cent, or 16 per cent compounded annually. From December, 1954, to November, 1955, the cost of living in Rio went up 30 per cent. Meanwhile, wages lagged far behind for most workers, though some of the new industrial workers gained.

The largest single drain on Brazil's foreign exchange is caused by the imports of petroleum, since the country produces only about 3 per cent of its requirements (1956). About $275 million annually are consumed by these imports, and the needs in recent years have been increasing at a rate of 20 per cent per annum. Unfortunately, petroleum has become primarily a political rather than an economic issue, being the outstanding example of economic nationalism in Latin America today. Brazil does not have adequate capital or the technical know-how to develop in the near future its own probably extensive petroleum resources. As a result of ultranationalist agitation, aggravated by Communist pressure, all aspects of the petroleum industry in Brazil, except the distribution of imports, have been tightly nationalized. No foreigner, nor even a Brazilian married to a foreigner, may own stock in Petrobras, the national petroleum corporation. The large American and British oil companies have offered to undertake exploration and development at their own expense and to share production on a fifty-fifty basis with the Brazilian government—with, however, administrative control. This the Brazilians will not let them have. Brazilian leaders have been adversely impressed by the petroleum experiences of Mexico and Iran. They have not studied so closely those of Canada, Venezuela, or Bolivia, where private American interests have been invited to enter under favorable conditions. Recently a high-ranking Brazilian government official came to the United States to seek the cooperation of *smaller* American companies, on a "contract" rather than a "concession" basis. It is doubtful, however, whether great strides will be made in the near future in developing Brazil's petroleum resources. This is particularly evident from the estimate that an investment of $1 billion, over an unusually successful decade, with 70 to 80 per cent in foreign currency, would be necessary to achieve self-sufficiency.

President Kubitschek has formulated a program which certainly hits at the weak spots of the economy, though it appears somewhat overambitious. The heart of the program is to expand electric power capacity from 3 to 5 million kilowatts by 1960, at a cost of $300 million in imported equipment. He proposes to undertake a major highway and storage construction and ship purchase program; and to increase iron ore exports from 1,600,000 to 10 million tons. He will undoubtedly avoid tackling the petroleum issue directly, and may instead try to find some loophole for foreign capital to enter. Kubitschek stated, on his recent trip to the United States and Europe, that he wants foreign private capital to enter on a large scale.

As can well be imagined, the illegal Brazilian Communist Party (now estimated unofficially to have over 100,000 members) has been able to make considerable capital out of these economic stresses and social dislocations. In particular, the rising cost of living and the increasing pressures among organized labor groups have enabled it to gain important strongholds in the labor movement. It also has great influence among intellectuals and publishes more papers than any other single political party, apparently obtaining considerable financing without much difficulty. A vital asset to the party is its leader, Luis Carlos Prestes, a highly respected though mysterious figure, who has been in hiding since 1947 and is generally conceded to be the spiritual leader of South America's Communists.

In the light of all these considerations it is not surprising that foreign observers have differed in their assessments of Brazil's future. Are these problems merely the "growing pains" of a rapidly developing country, or are they deep underlying maladies? Perhaps too much attention was focused during 1956 on what were essentially short-range problems. Yet one could not help noting some adverse underlying trends. The new economic and social groups which have appeared in recent years have continued largely to have the traditional orientation, especially in their desire for social status primarily and in their aversion to manual labor. There is a lack of agreement among the various economic, social, and regional interests as to how they should share equitably the burdens of rapid economic development. Perhaps the crux of the problem is that each group is reluctant to accept the reduced rate of consumption growth implied in the high rate of investment. There does seem to be, in other words, need for a *coordinated* will to develop.

Brazilian-American political relations since World War II have been harmonious. Unlike Argentina, Brazil has been the traditional friend and ally of the United States. In both world wars Brazil declared war on the enemies of the United States, and gave it active support. Since then, Brazilians, true to their reputations as skilled diplomats, have rendered valuable aid, both in the United Nations and the Organization of American States, as conciliators and moderators. Wary of Argentine motives, the other South American nations have generally been willing to follow Brazil's lead. Brazilians have complained that their long-term pro-American orientation has caused their country to be taken for granted by the United States, and some have facetiously suggested that Brazil should cause more trouble for the United States, as did Perón, in order to gain more attention and aid.

Not surprisingly, postwar Brazilian-American relations have been cast primarily in economic molds, though as we shall see, other than purely economic objectives are also at stake. Foremost is the fact that the United States is by far the largest purchaser of Brazil's coffee, to an amount in 1956 of around $1 billion. Large-scale governmental and private bank loans have been made to Brazil, the largest total to any Latin American country, though not so large as the Brazilians have felt they need and could successfully utilize. In addition, Brazil has received the largest single amount of Point Four aid in Latin America, during the years 1954-1956 about $3 million annually, or about one-eighth of the Latin American total. Point Four technical assistance was concentrated primarily, and by far most successfully, in the field of health and sanitation. Programs have also been established in vocational education,

196

public administration, and agriculture. Cutting across all these fields was the largest Point Four trainee program in Latin America, involving the dispatch of sizable numbers of Brazilians to the United States.

Actually, however, systematic, carefully planned economic aid on a really substantial scale commenced only in 1951. In the immediate postwar years Brazil, like the rest of Latin America, received scant attention. In 1948 a Joint Brazil-United States Technical Mission (generally referred to as the Abbink Mission) spent seven months in Brazil making an excellent survey of the nation's economic problems and needs, but no action was taken on it. Finally in 1951, largely through the vision of the late Francis Adams Truslow, then president of the New York Curb Exchange, and Assistant Secretary for Inter-American Affairs Edward Miller, it was recognized that Brazilian stability and progress are the cornerstone of American foreign-policy objectives in South America. A Joint Brazil-United States Economic Development Commission was established with headquarters in the huge Ministry of Finance building in Rio de Janeiro.* From 1951 to 1953 this group laid out a program for economic development and projects involving $300 million in loans from the World Bank and Export-Import Bank, the majority of which were to be in transportation and power.

The program was temporarily frustrated by an inflammatory speech by President Vargas, on January 1, 1952, charging foreign concerns (which meant in effect American) with "robbing" Brazil, by the abuse of a legislative provision allowing remittance of profits up to 8 per cent. (Vargas was to repeat this charge of exploitation in his suicide note.) Many companies had apparently invested comparatively little initially, but were now remitting their profits calculated on a much larger capital base, reflecting their reinvested profits. Alarmed by what seemed to be a new policy hostile to private foreign investment, the World Bank, dependent (as few Brazilians realized) on the private bond market for much of its capital, delayed for several months any loans to Brazil. The commission

*The author was a member of this Joint Commission.

and its program were on the verge of complete collapse, when at last the Export-Import Bank granted a number of loans, though the total amount was not nearly so great as the Brazilians (and some Americans) had expected.

The program of the joint commission was completed by July, 1953, but as late as September, 1956, the Brazilians complained that the World Bank had let them down. The Export-Import Bank had approved all seven loans referred to it, totaling $82.5 million, whereas the World Bank had approved only seven loans. totaling $89 million, out of twenty-four submitted to it, and amounting to $299 million. Unfortunately the Export-Import Bank in the period 1951-1954 had not yet begun to expand its Latin American lending operations. Most of the loans were referred to the World Bank, which was preoccupied with many other parts of the world, but in fairness we should note that up to April, 1956, the World Bank had loaned Brazil $194 million, which was 8.9 per cent of all money loaned by the bank, and 33.6 per cent of all loans made to Latin American countries. Yet it seemed in 1956 that one of Brazil's most important objectives should be to convince the World Bank that it was a good credit risk.

Patently this conflict involved higher national political and strategic interests, private business, and the lending objectives of an international institution. Vargas had obviously made his misleading, ill-timed speech in an effort to recoup his sinking political fortunes by a strong appeal to nationalism—not a surprising move, given the political situation of Brazil at that time. The question was whether the whole joint commission's program was to be treated as a purely business proposition, or was to be viewed as an effort to retrieve the Brazilian transportation system, principal backbone of the country's economic life, from almost sheer collapse and thereby help maintain Brazil as an invaluable friend and ally of the United States. German interests were already beginning to move into Brazil and would probably be quite willing to help develop the huge country and tie it in with German-made capital goods. The Soviet bloc, for political reasons, might be willing to offer some aid. These considerations, of course, did not greatly concern the World Bank, preoccupied with world-wide needs, but American foreign-policy officials should have discerned more quickly than they did that it was at bottom a matter of high-level American national interest. Not all the loan projects need have been approved automatically, but the whole problem should have been construed in the broad terms indicated above.

There were encouraging signs in 1956 that the United States was moving towards more aid to Brazil. In early 1956 an Export-Import Bank loan of $35 million was extended to the Brazilian national steel mill at Volta Redonda. Soon after the Panama Conference in July, 1956, the same bank extended loans amounting to $150 million, chiefly to improve the railway system. These loans were made largely as a result of Brazil's having achieved a favorable balance of payments through the curtailing of imports, thus indicating that it could help itself by adopting retrenchment measures. Now the problem of how to attract greatly increased private American capital remained. In 1954-1955, only a trickle, relatively speaking, had been going into Brazil. Private capital entry from Europe, for instance, was 75 per cent higher.

Two other types of economic relationship deserve special mention. In the latter part of 1955, the United States agreed to sell Brazil $41,220,000 worth of surplus wheat and other farm products, payable in cruzeiros, on what amounts to a forty-year credit. After petroleum, wheat imports were at this time the most serious drain on Brazil's inadequate foreign-exchange income. The original idea had been to keep Brazil from using up its short supply of dollars and at the same time enable the United States to use cruzeiros for purchase of strategic materials (especially manganese) for stockpiling. Nationalists and Communists, however, stimulated such strong opposition to alleged American efforts to plunder Brazil's strategic resources that the transaction was radically altered. Under the new arrangement, the United States would lend to Brazil 76 per cent of the proceeds of the sales at interests varying from 3 to 5 per cent, the loan to be repaid within 40 years. Meanwhile, Brazil would use those cruzeiros through her National Bank for Economic Development to finance long-range projects. The remaining 24

199

per cent of the cruzeiros would be used to finance United States operations in Brazil, such as expenses of the United States embassy and other agencies, purchases of strategic materials for stock-piling in the United States, "activities related to the expansion and distribution of agricultural products in Brazil," and expansion of the program of cultural interchange. Such an agreement served pressing needs of both countries well, and obviated the perennial dollar shortage.

The second economic relationship, one with obvious tremendous potential, involved an agreement between the two countries on the sharing of atomic know-how. Brazil would trade some of its thorium-bearing monazite sands for American technical knowledge and a reactor. For a while the agreement seemed to flounder on the shoals of nationalism, but finally its implementation appeared realizable.

As for the other countries in Latin America, we must ask what the general objectives of the United States' long-range Brazilian policy should be. Primary should be to keep Brazil, the bulwark of inter-American relations, strong. It is the bulwark for several reasons. In the first place, politically it has been and continues to be invaluable to the United States in dealing with the other Latin American nations. Secondly, its strategic "bulge" location, though not so crucial as during World War II, still appears to be the key to defense of the South American continent. Thirdly, within the next few years Brazil should become the outstanding economic power of Latin America. Finally, unlike Argentina, Brazil has in the modern era never shown itself to be aggressive or totalitarian, notwithstanding the pseudo-Fascist trappings under the Vargas dictatorship. Indeed its humanistic, racially tolerant way of life seems well suited for the Latin American area, and like the Mexican Indianist civilization, the kind of orientation conducive to harmony throughout Latin America.

In order for Brazil to be strong and at the same time continue to have a representative political system, it must not unduly restrain its rapid economic expansion. The country's economy cannot become static; political and social pressures are too great. In order to continue its economic growth, Brazil will need periodic American aid for the next several years. At the same time American leaders should urge their Brazilian counterparts to introduce at least some "austerity" measures, to help themselves as much as possible, for complete psychological dependence on American loans and other outside help is unhealthy. Moreover, economic aid is not enough. Brazil should continue to be consulted on prospective decisions in the United Nations and the Organization of American States. More attention should be paid in this country to the truly impressive cultural contributions of Brazil to the civilization of the New World, and the Brazilian-American exchange training and fellowship program should be continued and improved. One of the greatest single needs is for more young Americans to learn Portuguese and become thoroughly versed in Brazilian culture. Greatly augmenting fulfillment of this need would be establishment of an Institute of Brazilian Studies in some cosmopolitan center of the northeastern United States, where most of the Brazilian political, economic, and cultural interest is concentrated. A relatively few individuals with a good background in Brazilian studies, inside and outside our government service, can be of immense value in improving American relations with the country that is "half a continent."

Strongly oriented toward Brazil as it is, the United States should not forget that it also has important relations with Argentina. It would be most unwise to devote American attention to Brazil to the exclusion of its southern rival. Constant favoring of the huge Portuguese-speaking nation would cause the United States difficulties in its relations, not only with Argentina, but with other Latin American countries. In reality there seems little danger of this; the real problem is the reverse—taking Brazil for granted.

Is there any sense of balance of power, of conflicting interests, between the two large southern nations? History shows that during the period of the two Brazilian empires (1822-1889), Argentina and Brazil held rival spheres of influence in neighboring South American countries, although relations improved following the overthrow of the Empire. Certainly there are competing spheres of economic influence in Bolivia, Paraguay, Uruguay, and Peru. It is only natural that the two major powers of Latin America, expanding economically, would rub against each other from time to time. Argentina has shown more "dynamism" in its Latin American relations than Brazil, but one should not make the mistake of underrating the ability of the more "passive" Brazilians to uphold their interests. Thus there is a kind of balance of power. Yet the two economies do not compete. Argentina wheat is exchanged for Brazilian rubber and coffee and there is little competition of exports for Latin American or other foreign markets. Though many Brazilians dislike the "superior" Argentines, and many of the latter tend to look down on Brazilians, these attitudes should not be exaggerated. With Perón removed from the scene there are no ideological differences between the two countries.

In a way Brazil, often called the "land of the future," epitomizes Latin America. Great care has been taken in this book to avoid the often-heard lyrical panegyrics on the economic potential of Latin America. Yet one should also avoid the other extreme of negative pessimism. Brazil does have immense possibilities that are being realized, though not so rapidly as impatient Americans would like. As the country develops, it will become more and more important, not only on the Latin American but also on the world scene. In the opinion of most careful observers, Brazil rather than Argentina is the long-range key to influence and control in South America. The Germans and Japanese clearly understand this, and undoubtedly so does the Soviet bloc. The question is whether Americans also understand it. In this one area, the issues are not of a "crisis" or sensational nature and in that respect differ from the other three countries we have analyzed. Yet the long-run rewards are potentially the greatest of all and can be reaped by skillful wielding of American diplomacy, economic aid, and ideological influence. Yankee intervention need not be part of the problem at all.

-XIII-

Reflections on the Future

Perhaps readers will not be too disappointed to note that at this point we do not have a magic blueprint for a future Latin American policy. It is tempting indeed to speculate on the existence of such a plan, which would usher in a new period of harmony of the "good partner," to take its place with the earlier Good Neighbor epoch as a major landmark in inter-American good will. In our view, no such panacea exists.

But if a magic blueprint were available, would it stand any real chance of realization? The archives are full of grandiose schemes for improving general and specific aspects of inter-American relations which have never been carried out. It seems a foregone conclusion that, during our lifetime, there will be continued tension in Asia, the Near East, and North Africa, areas much closer than Latin America to the immediate military and strategic interests of the United States. This will undoubtedly mean continued priority preoccupation under any administration in Washington with those critical regions, as well as with the Soviet-Chinese blocs and Western Europe. In fact, in its "strategic loneliness," Latin America seems to have for company among the major regions only Central Africa and possibly Australia and New Zealand. This applies with particular force to central and southern *South* America.

A retrospective glance reveals that Latin America has since World War II been for the most part a noncontroversial, bipartisan area in American foreign policy. Neither Democratic nor Republican administrations paid much attention in their high-level political and diplomatic thinking to Latin America. In the election campaign of 1952, John Foster Dulles stated that adverse trends in Latin America made that area appear somewhat like China of the 1930's— certainly a provocative statement, leading some optimists to believe that considerably more attention would be paid to Latin America by the Republicans. They were disappointed. The new administration found itself overtaken by the pressure of deteriorating trends in the crisis areas of the world. The Guatemalan upset stimulated a little high-level thinking, as did the stresses and strains in Peronist Argentina. But the diversion of attention southward was actually resented by most harassed foreign-policy officials.

Probably this situation will not change substantially in the foreseeable future. Definite attention to Latin American policy will be paid only at times of revolutions or especially difficult problems involving specific countries. In other words the approach will be sporadic and empirical, one which has, by the way, been largely responsible for a curious phenomenon in inter-American relations that might be called a "dichotomy of the soul." On the one hand, flowery expressions of friendship are exchanged at Pan-American meetings and banquets, where all is sweetness and light. On the other hand, the real feelings of resentment at alleged neglect of many Latins are expressed "privately and informally" to journalists or individual Americans in academic and professional circles. This naturally leads to a boredom and cynicism at many Pan-American meetings and certainly does not generate dynamic interest. Dichotomy of this sort naturally exists for other areas, but it seems to be sharper for Latin America.

We venture to make a few more predictions, most of them along sobering, though by no means entirely pessimistic, lines. In the next decade or so, political instability and the ups and downs of dictatorships and democracies in Latin America will probably continue. Hopeful progress will appear to be made in some countries toward the evolution of a more truly democratic government, only to be counterbalanced by seeming reversions to repressive regimes in others. Yankeephobia will probably remain at least as strong as it is now; it may increase in certain areas. Dictators, exiles, ultranationalists, and other extreme partisans will continue to criticize the United States in bitter terms (on or off the record) for its policies, but for sharply differing reasons. The exiles, almost all of whom call themselves "liberals," will complain that the democratic United States is cynically supporting dictatorship in Latin America. By the same token, dictators and "conservatives" will often criticize Americans for having a superior attitude about their form of government and wanting to impose it on Latin America. They believe that those Latin Americans who prefer authoritarian government should not be criticized.

Economics will probably continue to dominate the thinking of most people, north and south, concerning United States-Latin American relations. Latin Americans will be preoccupied primarily with marketing their exports in the United States and with obtaining more intergovernmental loans, in order to obtain dollars for the coveted goal of economic development. American government officials and private businessmen will be more concerned with fostering a propitious climate in Latin America for foreign private investments and also, of course, with maintaining a good share of the Latin American market. Probably Export-Import Bank loans will be expanded, but there will never be enough government loans to satisfy the Latin American countries, especially the more rapidly growing ones like Brazil. Point Four will probably continue on a slightly expanded basis in various fields of activity, with improvements in administration of the program. Thus, economics will continue to be a very controversial field as well as a prevalent one. For example, charges of discrimination on tariffs will be made, and sharply differing interpretations as to the role of government in economic development will be offered. As to the future flow of private investment, it is hard to prognosticate. A guess is that American companies anxious to make profitable investments abroad will tend to favor this hemisphere and will simply adapt themselves as much as possible to the prevailing nationalistic restrictions which will in large part continue. As we indicated in Chapter VII, good public- and employee-relations programs will contribute materially to this adaptation.

As for ideological relations, always a nebulous sphere, some improvement may be hoped for, though nothing sensational. Perhaps the most encouraging factors are the steadily increasing numbers of Latin Americans coming to the United States, where they may see, at firsthand, life in their great northern neighbor. Especially the students may come to know the United States more profoundly through their years at the universities. Greatly improved air travel will facilitate these visits, as it will also increase travel to South America by Americans.

We do not envisage, then, any master policy plan. Within the realistic framework of probable future conditions thus outlined, however, certain kinds of direction should prove the most fruitful. Most significantly, perhaps, high-level foreign-policy officials should devote more consistent attention to long-range trends and underlying factors in Latin America. First place for such attention would be too much to ask, but let it not always be last. At the intermediate and lower levels, more men and women should be encouraged to enter government agencies. The government should take the initiative, for example, in recruiting from academic circles not just neophytes but also older people experienced in the Latin American field to serve with the agencies. There is a reservoir here—substantial in relation to the need—of talent available for Latin American service. Businessmen with Latin American involvement should be encouraged to meet periodically with government and academic specialists on Latin America to discuss underlying trends. Foundations, the main source of funds for area studies, might well consider turning a more receptive ear than they have in the past to requests for Latin American projects, and business groups might also consider granting subsidies for academic area programs.

The end objective is to have a group of people genuinely interested in, and with considerable knowledge of, Latin America. They will not simply be "marking time" until they can be sent to Europe and Asia. These people must speak Spanish and, if possible, Portuguese fluently, a prerequisite for real success in the Latin American diplomatic field, no matter what some may say. Latin America offers real scope for diplomatic skill, especially the ability, as one Latin put it, to say "no" gracefully to requests for loans.

An alert corps of officials dealing with Latin American policy will perceive that in the next decade Latin Americans will no longer be satisfied with merely "good will" on the part of Yankees. They will want moral, political, and economic guidance. This the United States must give. Let some say that it is a new kind of "imperialism" —they will say it no matter what the United States does.

The necessary guidance can probably best be furnished through the Organization of American States. True, bilateral negotiations will still be valuable, and loans and Point Four should still come to a great extent unilaterally from the United States. But the multilateral approach is an indispensable one. Thus far the OAS has been used mainly in settling disputes and in organizing hemispheric defense. With conditions reasonably peaceful, it seems to lose much of its reason for existing. Reinvigoration may be achieved by expanding the scope of the OAS to deal, in actuality, with many of the economic, social, and technical problems besetting the Latin American republics, instead of just writing reports about them.

At this writing the prospects seem encouraging. When the inter-American presidents met in July, 1956, in Panama, President Eisenhower suggested that a new group should be established, containing a representative from each republic, to prepare concrete recommendations for making the OAS more effective in fields affecting the welfare of peoples. The recommendations, the President continued, should include *practical* suggestions in economic, financial, social, and technical fields, and one of these might well be the beneficial use of nuclear forces throughout the hemisphere. Eisenhower's proposal seems to place a new emphasis on the dignity of the human being, not so much political but rather economic and social. One does not have to subscribe to the concept of "technocracy" used by Dr. Vallenilla Lanz to describe the Pérez Jiménez dictatorship in Venezuela in order to feel that it may be wiser to avoid the constant harping on political democracy for Latin America and instead to stress other kinds of human progress.

None of these measures will bring about the millennium. For example, no one should be so naive as to suppose that raising substantially the standard of living in Latin America will automatically cause Communist influence to become negligible. In industrializing countries like Brazil this influence will undoubtedly remain strong for some time to come. Furthermore, failure to provide for a steadily rising standard of living will certainly furnish a more fertile soil for the Communists to cultivate. People living in an atmosphere of constant economic insecurity and political instability tend to look toward extremist solutions, either of the left or of the right. Nevertheless, nationalism (stimulated by Communism), should be clearly pinpointed as the basic political trend of the future in Latin America.

Two exhortations seem pertinent. First, Americans should show more patience with Latin Americans than they ordinarily do. Considering the many obstacles—geographical, historical, and cultural —which the southern peoples have had to face, their progress has been significant. Second, Americans should not export their differences on foreign policy to Latin America. It is one thing to disagree with one another privately, but individuals on a government mission and even private businessmen abroad should hesitate to criticize adversely their country's policies. Most certainly government missions should not fight one another in the execution of policies. The British abroad have always shown a solidarity which is commendable.

It does seem clear that just because Latin America is rarely in the forefront of world news is no reason for taking it for granted. Hemispheric isolationism should be unequivocally rejected, but this does not mean that one should go to the other extreme. Regardless of the specific proposals recommended in this book, there will certainly have to be some farsighted thinking and vigorous, imaginative actions in our Latin American policy. If they are not adopted, and if the Soviet Union continues its economic and ideological offensive, Latin America may indeed within the next decade become estranged from the United States. The essential ingredient of mutual faith will have dissolved.

We have tried to avoid high-sounding phrases and empty oratory that are so often displayed by public speakers in discussing inter-American relations. Yet some lofty vision cannot be absent from our thoughts; otherwise there is no long-range goal and no meaning to the future. The following paragraph, excerpted from President

208

Eisenhower's address at the 1956 Panama meeting, conveys a fitting sense of destiny:

May it not be that we can now look forward to a new phase of association, in which we shall dedicate to individual human welfare the same measure of noble effort that, heretofore, has protected and invigorated the corporate life of our nations? I do not suggest that the initial task is ended. A nation's peace and liberty can never be taken for granted. We must constantly be vigilant, individually and collectively. But we can, I believe, in the coming years, concentrate more efforts to enriching the material, intellectual, and spiritual welfare of the individual.

Suggested Reading

(in English)

THE DEARTH OF BOOKS OR ARTICLES dealing with United States-Latin American relations since World War II is in itself a striking illustration of the lack of serious effort in this field. In fact, if it were not for the four excellent works in the American Foreign Policy Library—published by Harvard University Press—on relations between the United States and selected countries or regions in Latin America, there would be practically a blank. Sumner Welles is the editor and Donald McKay the associate editor of the series.

The four books are listed here. Each contains critical bibliographies.

CLINE, Howard F., *The United States and Mexico* (1953).

PERKINS, Dexter, *The United States and the Caribbean* (1947).

WHITAKER, Arthur P., *The United States and South America: The Northern Republics* (1948).

———, *The United States and Argentina* (1954).

Four additional works which cast light on interesting aspects of inter-American relations are:

CABOT, John Moors, *Toward Our Common American Destiny* (Medford, Mass.: Fletcher School of Law and Diplomacy, 1955). A collection of speeches and interviews by the former Assistant Secretary of State for Inter-American Affairs.

DUGGAN, Laurence, *The Americas: The Search for Hemisphere Security* (New York: Henry Holt and Co., 1949).

DEL RIO, Angel, ed., *Responsible Freedom in the Americas* (Garden City: Doubleday and Co., 1955).

WHITAKER, Arthur P., *The Western Hemisphere Idea: Its Rise and Decline* (Ithaca: Cornell University Press, 1954).

Though published in 1943, the following work addresses itself to the controversial problems of Yankee intervention and "imperialism" in Latin America up to that time, and has pertinence for the contemporary period on these issues:

BEMIS, Samuel F., *The Latin American Policy of the United States* (New York: Harcourt, Brace and Co., 1943).

Two interesting and provocative treatments by Latin Americans are:

DAVILA, Carlos, *We of the Americas* (New York: Ziff-Davis, 1949). Dávila, now deceased, was the former Secretary General of the Organization of American States.

ARCINIEGAS, Germán, *The State of Latin America* (New York: Alfred A. Knopf, Inc., 1952). Former Minister of Education of Colombia, Arciniegas is one of the leading liberal exiles in New York. His interpretation is strongly slanted from the traditional Latin American liberal point of view.

SUGGESTED READING

The following specialized books and articles were found particularly fruitful for the separate chapters.

CHAPTER III: TRENDS OF CONCERN: DICTATORSHIP, NATIONALISM, AND COMMUNISM

FITZGIBBON, Russell H., "How Democratic is Latin America?" *Inter-American Economic Affairs* (Spring, 1956).

KLING, Merle, "Towards a Theory of Power and Political Instability in Latin America," *The Western Political Quarterly*, IX (March, 1956).

STOKES, William S., "Violence as a Power Factor in Latin American Politics," *The Western Political Quarterly*, V, No. 3 (September, 1952). Excellent for its analysis of authoritarianism.

TANNENBAUM, Frank, "The Future of Democracy in Latin America," *Foreign Affairs*, XXXIII (April, 1955). Quite pessimistic in tone, but with a realistic ring.

CHAPTER IV: DEFINING YANKEE INTERVENTION

THOMAS, Ann van Wynen, and THOMAS, A. J., Jr., *Non-Intervention: The Law and Its Import in the Americas* (Dallas: Southern Methodist University Press, 1956). Mostly legalistic.

HANSON, Simon G., *Economic Development in Latin America* (Washington, D.C.: Inter-American Affairs Press, 1951). Pessimistic, controversial treatment, sharply critical at times of Latin American shortcomings, but provocative.

The Role of Universities in Technical Cooperation in Latin America (Washington, D.C.: National Planning Association, 1955).

CHAPTER VII: DYNAMISM OF PRIVATE ENTERPRISE

Three National Planning Association Case Studies of United States Business Performance Abroad:

WOOD, Richardson, *Sears, Roebuck de Mexico, S.A.* (Washington, D.C.: National Planning Association, 1953).

BURGESS, E. W., *Casa Grace in Peru* (Washington, D.C.: National Planning Association, 1954).

TAYLOR, W. C., *The Creole Petroleum Corporation in Venezuela* (Washington, D.C.: National Planning Association, 1955).

Somewhat uncritical in places, these publications contain most valuable data on this pioneering research topic.

CHAPTER IX: GUATEMALA: DILEMMA AND RESPONSIBILITY

GIBSON, John S., "The Guatemalan Case and Universal-Regional Relationships," *Foreign Affairs Reports*, IV, No. 1 (January, 1955).

GILLIN, John L., and SILVERT, K. H., "Ambiguities in Guatemala," *Foreign Affairs*, XXXIV (April, 1956).

JAMES, Daniel, *Red Design for the Americas: Guatemalan Prelude* (New York: John Day Co., 1954). Accurate on the part about Guatemala; the rest of the book is overly sensational, except for sound recommendations on United States policy in the last chapter.

TAYLOR, Philip B., Jr., "The Guatemalan Affair: A Critique of United States Foreign Policy," *The American Political Science Review* (September, 1956).

CHAPTER X: BOLIVIA: A CALCULATED RISK

OSBORNE, Harold, *Bolivia: A Land Divided* (London: Royal Institute of International Affairs, 1954).

212

UNITED NATIONS, Technical Assistance Administration, *Report on the United Nations Mission of Technical Assistance to Bolivia* (New York: United Nations, 1951).

CHAPTER XI: ARGENTINA: DESPITE PERON

BLANKSTEN, George, *Perón's Argentina* (Chicago: The University of Chicago Press, 1953). Good for an analysis of the Perón regime.

PENDLE, George, *Argentina* (London: Royal Institute of International Affairs, 1955).

WHITAKER, Arthur P., *The Argentine Upheaval* (New York: Praeger, 1956). Post-Perón Argentina and its relations with the United States.

CHAPTER XII: BRAZIL: A BULWARK TAKEN FOR GRANTED

CAMACHO, J. A., *Brazil: An Interim Assessment* (London: Royal Institute of International Affairs, 1952).

LIPSON, Leslie, "Government in Contemporary Brazil," *Canadian Journal of Economics and Political Science,* XXII (May, 1956).

Report of the Joint Brazil-United States Economics Development Commission (Washington, D.C.: Institute of Inter-American Affairs, 1953).

There is nothing more valuable than careful coverage of the *New York Times* daily and Sunday editions to keep abreast of Latin American political and economic developments. Also, the *Christian Science Monitor* contains interesting interpretations and background articles. *Time,* especially in its Latin American edition, has comparatively good coverage of Latin American news. *The Americas,* a monthly issued by the Pan American Union, has articles on current Latin American subjects of a popular and semipopular nature.

Inter-American Economic Affairs, edited by Simon G. Hanson, is the only scholarly magazine which is fully devoted to modern Latin America and inter-American relations. Though most of its articles are economic in nature, there are occasional political topics. *Hispanic American Historical Review* contains book reviews which are of particular interest.

Official publications of particular use include those of the United Nations, especially the Economic Commission for Latin America (Economic and Social Council); the Organization of American States and its secretariat, the Pan American Union; and the United States Department of State, the Department of Commerce, and the United States Information Agency. Valuable statistics, many of which were drawn upon in this book, are available in these publications. The *New York Times* also contains especially useful statistical data.

Index

ACT of Chapultepec, 63-64
Act of Havana, 63
Africa: Latins fear future of, 85
Agrarian reform: in Guatemala, 136-137, 143, 150; in Bolivia, 162, 165-166
"Agrarian Scissors of Latin America," 98-99, 101
"American": term defined, 1n
American business, in Latin America, 14-15, 23-24, 103; employment by, 106, 108-109, 135; operations of, 108-113 passim, 183
American Federation of Labor (AFL), 56, 138-139
American foreign relations: support by Latin diplomats, 27; in Guatemala, 155-157; in Bolivia, 169-173; in Argentina, 179-188; in Brazil, 196-202
Arbenz, Jacobo, 69, 136, 137, 139, 143, 144, 146, 150, 151, 154
Arbenz, María Cristina, 44
Arévalo, Juan José, 71, 136, 139, 144
Argentina: in world politics, 5-6; americanismo policy of, 25, 50; Soviet trade deals, 97; land and people, 174; Communist Party of, 176; rule by military junta, 177-178; and inter-American relations, 178-179, 181-182, 184-185
Atlantic Charter, 135
Atomic energy: fissionable materials, in South America, 21; and Latin America, 28-29; Brazilian agreement, 200

BAKER, Edgar R., 115
"Blue Book" (Argentina), 179
Bogotazo, 35
Bolivia: Communism in, 43, 169-170; economic considerations in, 53, 54, 158-160; politico-social background, 57, 158-161 passim; Point Four grants to, 89, 159n, 160n, 171; American

gifts to, 94; tin expropriation, 113, 165
Bolivian Socialist Falange (FSB), 162, 171
Braden, Spruille, 51, 57, 139, 179, 186, 187
Brazil, 32; nationalism and oil, 40; and Communism, 42, 44, 97-98, 192, 195; economic aid to, 55, 196-200; and American private investment, 104; land and people, 189-190; historical past, 190-192, 201; economic problems of, 193-196; Point Four aid, 196-197

CAPEHART Report, 164n
Caracas Declaration, 68, 141-142
Castillo Armas, Carlos, 147-154
Chile, 32; and Communism, 42-43, 44; American gifts to, 94
Christian Science Monitor, 10, 14, 139
Church and State, Latin America, 32, 43-44, 138, 162
Clark Memorandum, 51
Colombia, 32, 43, 67
Colonization plans: in Guatemala, 150; in Bolivia, 168
Communism, 31, 34; and Latin exiles, 36; and Latin America today, 40-45, 52, 67-68. See also individual countries
Costa Rica, 32, 55; dispute with Nicaragua, 56-57, 72-77. See also Figueres, José
Cuba, 48-49, 98

DARIO, Rubén, 48, 121
Declaration of Lima, 62
Dictatorship, Latin American: trends, 31-37, 44, 58, 191; and foreign economic relations, 38-39; American policy toward, 57-59; predictions on, 204-205

215